A Manual of Special Education Law for Educators and Parents

M. Jean Rawson, ESQ.

Morgen Publishing, Inc.

Copyright © 2000 by Morgen Publishing, Inc.

ISBN: 0-9676206-0-0

Library of Congress Catalog Card Number: 99-091377

All rights reserved. No part of this publication may be reproduced, stored in a retrieval system, or transmitted, in any form or by any means, electronic, mechanical, photocopying, recording, or otherwise, without the prior written permission of the publisher.

Printed in the United States of America

Published by
Morgen Publishing, Inc.
P.O. Box 754
Naples, Florida 34102
Phone: 941-263-8206
Fax: 941-263-8472
E-mail: Mjrmickey@aol.com

Cover and Interior Design and Production: Gene Crofts

First Edition
Printing 10 9 8 7 6 5 4 3 2 1

Dedicated to
the special education students of America

In memory of
Marjorie J. Rawson

who listens to the "music not yet written."
Alice Walker

*To Dr. Fitzgerald —
Thank you for your
interest in my book — and
for your dedication
special education!
Sincerely,
M. Jean Rawson
January 2000*

Contents

Cases	ix
Preface	xvii
About the Author	xix

Chapter 1

Introduction 1

Chapter 2

Definitions 5

Assistive Technology Device	5
Assistive Technology Service	6
Child with a Disability	7
Consent	8
Day	9
Extended School Year	9
Free Appropriate Public Education (FAPE)	10
General Curriculum	11
Individualized Education Program (IEP)	12
Least Restrictive Environment (LRE)	12

Related Services	13
Medical Services	*13*
Transportation	*15*
Special Education	16
Stay Put	17
Supplementary Aids and Services	17
Transition Services	18

Chapter 3

Identification 21
Child Find 21

Chapter 4

Evaluation 23
Initial Evaluation 23
Re-Evaluation 25
Independent Educational Evaluation (IEE) 28

Chapter 5

Determination of Eligibility 31

Chapter 6

Individualized Education Programs 35
Overview 35
Content 36
Participation in Assessments 40
The IEP Team 41

Contents

Review and Revision of the IEP	47
IEP Meetings	48
Concensus	*48*
What Is NOT an IEP Meeting?	*49*
Recording Devices	50
Accountability	51

Chapter 7

Placement 55

Chapter 8

Discipline of a Student with a Disability 59

Placement in an Alternative Educational Setting	61
Functional Behavioral Assessments	67
Behavior Intervention Plans	70
Manifestation Determination Hearings	75
Entitlement to Protections	78
Inmate Services	80
Referral to Law Enforcement	81

Chapter 9

Procedural Safeguards 83

Written Notice	83
Content of the Notice	84
Transfer of Rights	85
Graduation	86

Chapter 10
Mediation 89

Chapter 11
Due Process Hearings 93

Chapter 12
Attorneys' Fees 99

Chapter 13
Damages 103

Chapter 14
Charter Schools 105

Chapter 15
Children in Private Schools 107
    School-Placed   107
    Parentally Placed   108

Afterword 115
Index 117

Cases

Board of Education v. Rowley, 458 U.S. 176 102 S. Ct. 3034 (1982)	2
Letter to Kleczka, 30 **IDELR** 270 (OSEP 1998)	9
Ridgewood Bd. of Educ. v. N.E., 30 **IDELR** 41 (3d Cir. 1999)	11
Kari H. v. Franklin Spec. Sch. Dist, 16 **IDELR** 569 (6th Cir. 1997)	12
Hudson by Hudson v. Bloomfield Hills Pub. Schs., 26 **IDELR** 607 (6th Cir. 1997)	13
Hartmann by Hartmann v. Loudoun County Bd. of Educ., 26 **IDELR** 167 (4th Cir. 1997)	13
Irving Independent School District v. Tatro (468 U.S. 883 (1984)	13
Cedar Rapids Community School District v. Garret F. (No. 96-1793, decided March 3, 1999)	14
Letter to Smith, 23 **IDELR** 344 (OSEP 1995)	15
Brent v. San Diego Unified Sch. Dist., 25 **IDELR** 344 (S.D. Calif. 1996)	15
San Diego Unified Sch. Dist., 28 **IDELR** 244 (SEA CS 1998)	15
Board of Education of the Roslyn Union Free School District, 27 **IDELR** 1113 (SEA NY 1998)	15

A Manual of Special Education Law

Malehorn v. Hill City Sch. Dist., 27 IDELR 144 (S.D. 1997)	16
Highland Local Sch. Dist., 26 IDELR 224 (SEA Ohio 1997)	16
Shasta Union H.S. Dist., 30 IDELR 733 (SEA CA 1999)	28
Lewisville Independent Sch. Dist., 28 IDELR 1024 (SEA TX 1998)	28
Oregon City Sch. District 62, 28 IDELR 536 (SEA ORE 1998)	28
San Antonio Independent Sch. Dist., 29 IDELR 630 (SEA TX 1998)	29
Long Beach Unified School Dist., 28 IDELR 777 (SEA CA 1998)	29
Board of Educ. of the Victor Central Sch. Dist., 27 IDELR 1159 (SEA NY 1998)	29
West Contra Costa Unified School District, 28 IDELR 802 (SEA CA 1998)	29
Community Consolidated School Dist. No. 180, 27 IDELR 1004 (SEA Ill. 1998)	30
Letter to Anonymous, 30 IDELR 538 (OSEP 1998)	32
O'Toole by O'Toole v. Olathe District Sch. Unified Sch. District No. 233, 28 IDELR 177 (10th Cir., 1998)	36
Greenbush Sch. Committee v. Mr. And Mrs. K. ex. rel. JK, 26 IDELR 200 (D. Me. 1996)	41
O'Toole by O'Toole v. Olathe District Sch. Unified Sch. Dist. No 233, 28 IDELR 177 (10th Cir., 1998)	41
Gwinnett Country School System, 4 ECLPR, Sec. 98 (SEA Ga., 1999)	43
Amanda S. by Susan S. v. Webster City Community School District, 27 IDELR 698 (N.D. Iowa 1998)	43

Cases

Three Rivers/Josephine County School District, 28
    IDELR 1228 (SEA OR 1998)   43

Searcy Public Schools, 30 IDELR 825 (SEA AR 1999)   44

Letter to Collins, 30 IDELR 404 (OSEP 1998)   46

McMillan by Collins v. Cheatham County Schools, 25 IDELR
    398 (M.D. Tenn. 1997)   47

Letter to Slatkin, 213:128, OSERS 1998   48

Letter to Blades, 213:169, OSERS, 1988   49, 50

Cronkite v. Long Beach Unified Sch. Dist., 30 IDELR 510
    (9th Cir., 1999)   51

*O'Toole by O'Toole v. Olathe Dist. Schs. Unified Sch. Dist.
    No. 233*, 28 IDELR 177 (10th Cir., 1998)   51

Tucson Unified Sch. Dist., 30 IDELR 478 (SEA Ariz., 1999)   52

*O'Toole by O'Toole v. Olathe Dist. Schs. Unified Sch. Dist.
    No. 233*, 28 IDELR 177 (10th Cir., 1998)   52

Tuscaloosa County School Board, 30 IDELR 842 (SEA AL 1999)   52

Dallas School District, 28 IDELR 1225 (SEA TX 1998)   56

*Morris by Morris v. Metropolitan Gov't of Nashville and
    Davidson County*, 26 IDELR 159 (M.D. Tenn. 1997)   56

Oberti v. Clemson Sch. Dist., 995 F. 2d 1204 (3rd Cir., 1993)
    19 IDELR 908   57

Letter to Hale, 30 IDELR 142 (OSEP 1997)   58

Sherry v. New York State Educ. Dept. 479 F. Supp. 1328
    (W.D.N.Y. 1979)   60

Buncombe County Sch. Dist., 23 IDELR 364 (OCR 1995)   60

District of Columbia Public Schools, 28 IDELR 401
    (SEA D.C. 1998)   60

Pottstown School Dist., 30 IDELR 651 (SEA PA 1999)   62

Letter to Bachman, 29 IDELR 1092 (OSEP, 1997)   63

Honig v. Doe, EHLR 559:231 (1988)   64

OSEP Memorandum, 26 IDELR 981(1997)   64

Gadsden City Board of Education v. B. P., 28 IDELR 166 (N.D. Ala. 1998)   64

Independent School Dist No. 279, Osseo Area School, 30 IDELR 645 (SEA MN 1999)   65

William S. Hart Union High School Dist., 26 IDELR 1258 (SEA Calif., 1997)   65

Community Consolidated School District 15, 30 IDELR 448, (SEA IL, 1999)   65

Bd. of Educ. Of the Akron Central School Dist., 28 IDELR 909 (SEA NY 1998)   66

Freeport Public Schools, 26 IDELR 1251 (SEA ME 1997)   66

Oregon City School Dist., 28 IDELR 96 (SEA OR 1998)   66

Pottstown School District, 30 IDELR 651 (SEA PA 1999)   67

Independent School District No. 2310, 29 IDELR 330 (SEA Minn. 1998)   68

William S. Hart Union High Sch. Dist., 26 IDELR 1258 (SEA CA 1997)   69

Bd. of Educ. Of the Akron Central Sch. Dist, 28 IDELR 909 (SEA NY 1998)   70

Independent School Dist. No. 2310, 29 IDELR 330 (SEA MN 1998)   70

Freeport Public Schools, 26 IDELR 1251 (SEA ME 1997)   74

Devine Independent School District, 25 IDELR 1238 (SEA Tex. 1997) — 74

Stroudsburg Area School District, 27 IDELR 975 (SEA Pa. 1997) — 74

Hacienda La Puente Unified School District, 30 IDELR 105 (SEA CA 1999) — 75

Horry County School District v. P.F., 29 IDELR 354 (D.S.C. 1998) — 75

Metropolitan Nashville (TN) Public Schools, 29 IDELR 488 (OCR 1998) — 75

Fairfax County Public Schools, 29 IDELR 1008 (SEA VA 1998) — 76

Northeast Independent School District, 28 IDELR 1004 (SEA TX 1998) — 76

In Re: Student with a Disability, 30 IDELR 113 (SEA CT 1999) — 77

Ashland Sch. Dist., 28 IDELR 630 (SEA Ore. 1998) — 78

North Pocono School District, 29 IDELR 111 (SEA PA 1998) — 79

Miller v. Board of Educ. of Caroline County, 25 IDELR 811 (Md. Ct. Spec. App. 1997) — 80

Rodiriecus L. v. Waukegan Sch. Dist., 24 IDELR 563 7th Cir., 1996) — 81

Board of Trustees of Target Range Sch. Dist. No. 23, 18 IDELR 1019 (9th Cir., 1992) — 85

Daugherty by Daugherty v. Hamilton County Schs., 26 IDELR 127 (E.D. Tenn. 1997) — 86

Independent School District No. 281 (Robbinsdale), 28 IDELR 370 (SEA MN 1998) — 90

Little Rock School District v. Mauney, 30 **IDELR** 668
(8th Cir. 1999) 93

Sherri A.D. v. Kirby, 19 **IDELR** 339 (5th
Cir. 1992) 93

Ojai Unified Sch. Dist. v. Jackson, 20 **IDELR** 354
(9th Cir. 1993) 95

*Logue by Logue v. Shawnee Mission Public Schs. Unified Sch.
Dist. No. 512*, 25 **IDELR** 587 (SEA Kan. 1997) 96

Board of Education of the Pittsford Central School Dist.,
29 **IDELR** 653 (SEA NY 1998) 96

Board of Education of the Jericho Union Free School District,
29 **IDELR** 135 (SEA NY 1998) 97

*Board of Education of the City School District of the City of
New York*, 27 **IDELR** 1000 (SEA NY 1998) 97

Dallas Independent School District, 29 **IDELR** 930 (SEA
TX 1998) 97

Board of Education of the Averill Park Central School District,
27 **IDELR** 996 (SEA N.Y. 1998) 97

Board of Education of the Canastota Central School District,
27 **IDELR** 419 (SEA NY 1997) 97

*Judith S. v. Board of Education of Community Unit School
District No. 200*, 28 **IDELR** 728 (ND Ill. 1998) 97

Dallas Independent School District, 29 **IDELR** 930 (SEA
TX 1998) 98

Pascoe v. Washington Central School District, 29 **IDELR** 31
(S.D. NY 1998) 98

*Board of Education of the City School District of the City of
Ithaca*, 28 **IDELR** 71 (SEA NY 1998) 98

Cases

Walled Lake Consolidated Schools by Jones by Thomas, 24 IDELR 738 (ED Mich. 1996)	98
Hensley v.Eckerhart, 461 U.S. 424 (1983)	100
Mr. and Mrs. H. v. Region Board of Education, 30 IDELR 359 (D. Conn. 1999)	100
Hall by Hall v. Vance County Bd. of Educ., 774 F. 2d 629 (4th Cir. 1985)	103
Humble Independent School District, 29 IDELR 833 (SEA TX 1998)	104
Charlie F. v. Board of Educ. of Skokie Sch. Dist., 98 F. 3d 989 (7th Cir. 1996). 24 IDELR 1039	104
W.B. v. Matula, 67 F. 3d 484, 23 IDELR 411 (3rd Cir. 1995)	104
Gupta v. Montgomery County Public Schools, 25 IDELR 115 (D. MD 1996)	104
Fort Zumwalt School District v. Clynes, et. al. 26 IDELR 172 (8th Cir. 1997)	104
Heidemann v. Rother, 84 F. 3d 1021, 24 IDELR 167 (8th Cir. 1996)	104
Letter to Burr, 30 IDELR 146, OSEP 1998	107
Letter to McKethan, 29 IDELR 907, OSEP 1998	108
Northwestern Lehigh School District, 29 IDELR 940 (SEA PA 1999)	108
Foley v. Special Sch. Dist. of St. Louis, 28 IDELR 874 (8th Cir., 1998)	108
Letter to McKethan, 29 IDELR 907, OSEP 1998	109
Goodall v. Stafford County Sch. Bd., 60 F. 3d 168, 22 IDELR 972 (4th Cir., 1995)	109

Russman by Russman v. Mills, 28 **IDELR** 612 (2d Cir. 1998)   109

Letter to Rothman, 30 **IDELR** 269, **OSEP** 1998   110

Cefalu ex. rel. Cefalu v. East Baton Rouge Parish Sch. Bd., 117 F. 3d 231 (5th Cir. 1997), 25 **IDELR** 142   110

K.R. v. Anderson Community Sch. Dist., 26 **IDELR** 864 (7th Cir. 1997)   111

South Lyon Community School, 30 **IDELR** 728 (SEA MI 1999)   111

Preface

> *"It's amazing what ordinary people can do if they set out without preconceived notions."*
> Charles F. Kettering

Unfortunately, special education is one of the most misunderstood and often one of the most legislated and litigated areas in public education. Necessarily, a knowledge of the legal requirements for special education is vital for educators, for parents, and for aspiring students majoring in special education.

The goal of this book, as a practical resource, is primarily one of problem prevention. It is also a source for current, critical legal information. Because it is a complete compilation of the most important parts of the 1997 Individuals with Disabilities Education Act, its implementing Regulations of 1999, and recent decisions interpreting the law, this book addresses the major aspects of special education law and its practical application for schools and parents. "Noteworthy" footnotes highlight each chapter to illustrate significant points of law.

Acquisition of legal information and a pro-active application of the law will prevent many difficulties that might otherwise occur between parents and educators. Well-reasoned decisions at IEP meetings that comply with the current federal law are essential to avoid friction, conflict, and inefficiency. Additionally, such knowledge will enable policies to be developed and decisions to be made that comply with current law, that avoid and limit costly litigation, and that will serve the best interests of children. This book promotes collaboration between educators and parents. A knowledge of the law empowers people, which will lead to understanding and cooperation. Nothing will "astonish others so much as common sense and plain dealing". (Ralph Waldo Emerson) The absence of preconceived notions by parents and educators will ultimately best serve both the needs of our society and the needs of our most important resource-our children.

Grateful acknowledgments to the following who have assisted with this project:

> Annette Kocal, Editor
> Dorothy DeMichele, DDP (Public Relations)
> Accent Print of Naples, Florida

> M. Jean Rawson, Esq.
> *November 1999*

About the Author

M. Jean Rawson, B.S., University of Mississippi; M.S., Indiana University; J.D., John Marshall Law School, Chicago, is admitted to practice law in Florida and Indiana in all state and federal courts and in the U.S. Supreme Court. A former high school teacher, Ms. Rawson has served as an adjunct professor of school law at Indiana University, Purdue University, University of South Florida, and John Marshall Law School. She served as an administrative hearing officer for the Indiana Department of Special Education and as the Compliance Specialist for the School District of Collier County, Florida. Ms. Rawson has a private law practice in Naples, Florida, concentrating in family law, juvenile law, school law, and special education law.

The hiring of a lawyer is an important decision that should not be based solely upon advertisements. Before you decide, ask us to send you free written information about our qualifications and experience.

Chapter 1

Introduction

"The only real disability is a bad attitude."
Unknown

Prior to the 1970's, there existed a philosophy that placed the burden of educating children with disabilities primarily on the family. A series of court decisions, the passage of federal laws, and other governmental involvement beginning in the 1970's dramatically altered the relationship between students with disabilities and public schools. The Elementary and Secondary Education Act was passed in 1965; Title VI amended the Act in 1966. In 1970, Title VI was repealed and replaced by the Education of the Handicapped Act of 1970, and a Bureau of Education for the Handicapped was created. In 1975, the Education for All Handicapped Children Act (P.L. 94-142) was passed under which federal funds subsidized special education in those states meeting qualification requirements. The

Education for All Handicapped Children Act required states to adopt policies that assured all handicapped children a "free appropriate public education". Later legislation employed the term "disabled" rather than "handicapped".

One of the major underlying principles of the Education for All Handicapped Children Act was that special education and related services granted to students with handicaps must be "appropriate". In 1982, the United States Supreme Court delivered a 6-3 decision that addressed the limitations of the Act's guarantees and attempted to define the term "appropriate." In *Board of Education v. Rowley*, 458 U.S. 176; 102 S. Ct. 3034 (1982), the Court held that a child was being provided an appropriate special education because the child was receiving personalized instruction with sufficient supportive services to permit her to benefit from the instruction. In addition, the school provided the program at public expense, the program approximated the child's age-appropriate grade level, the school complied with the IEP, and due process procedures were followed.

The Education for the Handicapped Act Amendments of 1990 gave the Act a new title—The Individual with Disabilities Education Act (IDEA). The language of IDEA used the term "disability" instead of "handicap" and the terms, "children with disabilities." In 1997, the Individual with Disabilities Education Act was amended. Technically considered a "reauthorization", the Individuals with Disabilities Education Act Amendments of 1997 were signed into law by President William J. Clinton on June 4, 1997. The Amendments constitute the most sweeping change in

Introduction

the law since the enactment of Public Law 94-142 in 1975. The Amendments, which clarify IDEA, significantly change a number of the policies, procedures, and practices regarding the education of students with disabilities.

The major themes of the Reauthorized IDEA:

A. Strengthening parental participation in the educational process;

B. Accountability for student participation in the general education curriculum and mastery of IEP goals and objectives;

C. Remediation and rehabilitation of behavior problems at school and in the classroom;

D. Preparation of students with disabilities for employment and independent living. OSERS *IDEA '97*

Issued two years later (May 11, 1999), the implementing Regulations for the Individuals with Disabilities Education Act Amendments of 1997 contain changes that touch every key aspect of special education law and practice. The purpose of the Regulations is to effectuate the requirements set forth in the 1997 IDEA Amendments by filling in some of the details which are necessary to carry out the mandates of the law. Case law has continued to further define both IDEA and the Regulations.

Student Artist: Sarina Lasko
Pine Ridge Middle School, Naples, Florida
Teacher: Carol Mullen

Chapter 2

Definitions

"The beginning of wisdom is the definition of terms."

Plato

IDEA and the Regulations define a number of terms. Understanding those terms will lead to a better understanding of what is required under the law.

Assistive Technology Device

Any item, piece of equipment, or product system, whether acquired commercially off the shelf, modified, or customized, that is used to increase, maintain, or improve functional capabilities of a child with a disability. 20 U.S.C. 1401 (1); 34 C.F.R. 300.5

Assistive Technology Service

Any service that directly assists a child with a disability in the selection, acquisition, or use of an assistive technology device. Such terms include:

the evaluation of the needs of such child, including a functional evaluation of the child in the child's customary environment;

purchasing, leasing, or otherwise providing for the acquisition of assistive technology devices by such child;

selecting, designing, fitting, customizing, adapting, applying, maintaining, repairing, or replacing of assistive technology devices;

coordinating and using other therapies, interventions, or services with assistive technology devices, such as those associated with existing education and rehabilitation plans and programs;

training or technical assistance for such child, or where appropriate, the family of such child; and

training or technical assistance for professionals (including individuals providing education and rehabilitation services), employers, or other individuals who provide services to, employ, or are otherwise substantially involved in the major life function of such child. 20 U.S.C. 1401 (2); 34 C.F.R. 300.6

Each school must ensure that assistive technology devices or assistive technology services, or both, are made available to a child with a disability if required as a part of the child's special education, related services, or supplementary aids and services. On a case-by-case basis, the use of school-purchased assistive technology devices in a child's home or in other settings is required if the child's IEP team determines that the child needs to access to those devices in order to receive FAPE. 34 C.F.R. 300.308

Child with a Disability

A child with mental retardation, hearing impairments (including deafness), speech or language impairments, visual impairments (including blindness), emotional disturbance, orthopedic impairments, autism, traumatic brain injury, other health impairments, or specific learning disabilities; and who, by reason thereof, needs special education and related services. 20 U.S.C. 1401 (3)

Children aged 3 through 9 may be classified as having developmental delays if they have significant cognitive disabilities, or any other disabilities as measured by appropriate diagnostic instruments and procedures, in one or more of the following areas: physical development, cognitive development, communication development, social or emotional development, or adaptive development; and if they, by reason thereof, need special education and related services. 20 U.S.C. 1401 (3)

Other health impairment means having limited strength, vitality or alertness, including a heightened alertness to environmental stimuli, that results in limited alertness with respect to the educational environment that is due to chronic or acute health problems such as attention deficit disorder or attention deficit hyperactivity disorder, and which adversely affects a child's educational performance. 34 C.F.R. 300.7 (c) (9)

Consent

> The parent has been fully informed of all information relevant to the activity for which consent is sought, in his or her native language, or other mode of communication;
>
> The parent understands and agrees in writing to the carrying out of the activity for which his or her consent is sought, and the consent describes the activity and lists the records (if any) that will be released and to whom; and
>
> The parent understands that the granting of consent is voluntary on the part of the parent and may be revoked.
>
> If a parent revokes consent, that revocation is not retroactive (i.e., it does not negate an action that has occurred after the consent was given and before the consent was revoked). 34 C.F.R. 300.500 (b) (1)

Informed parental consent must be obtained before conducting an initial evaluation or re-evaluation and before initial provision of special education and related services to a child with a disability. 34 C.F.R. 300.505 (a) (1)

Parental consent must also be obtained before personally identifiable information is disclosed to anyone other than officials of participating agencies collecting or using the information. C.F.R. 300.571 (a)

Definitions

Day

A calendar day unless otherwise indicated as business day or school day. 34 C.F.R. 300.9

Extended School Year (ESY)

Special education and related services that are provided to a child with a disability beyond the normal school year, in accordance with the child's IEP, and at no cost to the parents of the child. 34 C.F.R. 300.309 (b)

ESY services must be provided only if a child's IEP team determines, on an individual basis, that the services are necessary for the child to receive FAPE. A school may not limit ESY services to particular categories of disability or unilaterally limit the type, amount, or duration of the services. 34 C.F.R. 300.309 (a)

The Office of Special Education Programs has noted that there are two types of summer school programs—extended school year services and summer school. ESY are services provided during breaks in the academic year to students with disabilities on an individual need basis. Summer school is a separate program, which can be for any student. Whether a student with a disability requires ESY is a decision for the IEP team. Nothing in IDEA or the Regulations requires students with disabilities who do not meet their IEP goals to participate in ESY. *Letter to Kleczka*, 30 IDELR 270 (OSEP 1998)

Free Appropriate Public Education (FAPE)

"The entire object of true education is not merely to be learned, but to love knowledge."

John Ruskin

Special education and related services that (a) have been provided at public expense, under public supervision and direction, and without charge; (b) meet the standards of the State educational agency; (c) include an appropriate preschool, elementary, or secondary school education in the State involved; and (d) are provided in conformity with the individualized education program. 20 U.S.C. 1401 (8); 34 C.F.R. 300.13

Each state shall ensure that **FAPE** is available to any individual child with a disability who needs special education and related services, even though the child is advancing from grade to grade. 34 C.F.R.300.121 (e) (1)

A free appropriate public education is available to all children with disabilities between the ages of 3 and 21, inclusive, including children with disabilities who have been suspended or expelled from school. 20 U.S.C. 1412 (a) (1); 34 C.F.R. 300.300 (a) (1) **FAPE** need not be available to students with disabilities who have graduated with a regular high school diploma. However, **FAPE** must be made available to students who have graduated—but not with a regular diploma. 34 C.F.R. 300.122 (a) (3)

The standard for **FAPE** has been stated as follows: "The

IEP must offer an opportunity for 'significant learning and meaningful educational benefit'." *Ridgewood Bd. of Educ. v. N.E.*, 30 IDELR 41 (3d Cir. 1999)

In order to provide a free appropriate public education, services must address all of the child's identified special education and related services needs, and the services must be based on the child's unique needs and not on the child's disability. 34 C.F.R. 300.300 (a) (3)

General Curriculum

The same curriculum as for non-disabled students. 34 C.F.R. 300.347 (a)

General curriculum is a single curriculum adopted by the school district for all students from preschool through secondary school.

This term relates to the content of the curriculum and not to the setting in which it is used. Depending upon the individual needs of the student with a disability, and consideration of the least restrictive environment requirements, the general curriculum could be used for students with disabilities in any educational environment along the continuum of placements. The extent of involvement in the general curriculum should be considered for each student by the IEP team.*

---

*Individual Educational Plans and IDEA 1997, Technical Assistance Paper, Florida Department of Education, FY 1999-4-D, August 1998

Individualized Education Program (IEP)

"Long-range planning does not deal with future decisions, but with the future of present decisions."

Peter Drucker

A written statement for each child with a disability that is developed, reviewed, and revised. 20 U.S.C. 1401(11)

Least Restrictive Environment (LRE)

To the maximum extent appropriate, children with disabilities, including children in public or private institutions or other care facilities, are educated with children who are not disabled, and special classes, separate schooling, or other removal of children with disabilities from the regular educational environment occurs only when the nature or severity of the disability of a child is such that education in regular classes with the use of supplementary aids and services cannot be achieved satisfactorily. 20 U.S.C. 1412 (5) (A); 34 C.F.R.300.550

In *Kari H. v. Franklin Spec. Sch. Dist*, 16 IDELR 569 (6th Cir. 1997), the Court determined that the proposed district placement for a 14-year-old student with severe mental retardation in a self-contained special education class with partial mainstreaming was appropriate. The same Court found that the school district's program for a 14-year-old trainable mentally impaired student was appropriate since it provided for educational benefit in the least restrictive environment. *Hudson by Hudson v. Bloomfield Hills Pub. Schs.*, 26 IDELR 607 (6th Cir. 1997) The IDEA only creates a preference for mainstreaming, not a mandate. *Hartmann by Hartmann v. Loudoun County Bd. of Educ.*, 26 IDELR 167 (4th Cir. 1997).

Related Services

> Includes transportation, and such developmental, corrective, and other supportive services (including speech-language pathology and audiology services, psychological services, physical and occupational therapy, recreation, including therapeutic recreation, social work services, counseling services, including rehabilitation counseling, orientation and mobility services, and medical services (except that such medical services shall be for diagnostic and evaluation purposes only) as may be required to assist a child with a disability to benefit from special education, and includes the early identification and assessment of disabling conditions in children. 20 U.S.C. 1401 (22)

If it is determined through an appropriate evaluation that a child has one of the disabilities under IDEA, but only needs a related service and not special education, the child is NOT a child with a disability.

Medical Services are services provided by a physician. The *Irving Independent School District v. Tatro* (468 U.S. 883 (1984)) decision is known as the chief authority interpreting the term, "medical services". In the *Tatro* case, the Supreme Court used a two-step analysis to find that the law required the district to perform clean intermittent catheterization (CIC) for a student with a neurogenic bladder. First, the Court ruled that CIC is a supportive service because without it the student could not attend school or benefit from special education. Second, the Court adopted the "bright-line" rule suggested by the Department of Education's regulations which limits the medical exclusion to those services that must be performed by a physician or a hospital. Accordingly, as a school nurse could perform CIC, the Court held that it was not excluded as a medical service.

To reconcile the disparity in judicial interpretations that have emerged since the *Tatro* decision, the United States Supreme Court heard a case on medical services in 1999. In *Cedar Rapids Community School District v. Garret F.* (No. 96-1793, decided March 3, 1999), the Supreme Court ruled that IDEA requires schools to provide continuous care for a special education student so long as it does not include medical services performed by doctors. The student was paralyzed from the neck down due to a motorcycle accident and required services to repair the ventilator if it malfunctioned; to suction the tracheotomy tube as needed, but at least once every 6 hours; to assist with eating and drinking; to administer urinary bladder catheterization once a day; to place the student in a reclining position for 5 minutes each hour; and to respond in an emergency situation if the student experienced autonomic hyperreflexia. Citing the stated purpose of IDEA, the Court found that the district was

> ***Noteworthy***
>
> It is important to be able to speak and understand the language of special education.

obligated to provide the service in accordance with the "bright-line" view, because the requested services did not have to be provided by a physician.

Transportation is to include travel to and from school and between schools, travel in and around school building, and "specialized equipment" (such as special or adapted buses, lifts and ramps), if required to provide a special education for a student with a disability. 34 C.F.R. 300.24 (b) (14)

School districts must provide transportation to students with disabilities if they provide transportation to the general student population. In the event that a school does not supply transportation to its general population, then the issue of transportation for students with disabilities must be decided on a case-by-case basis. Like other related services, if transportation is required for a student to benefit from special education, it must be provided at no cost to parents. *Letter to Smith*, 23 IDELR 344 (OSEP 1995)

The duty to transport is not limited to the day's beginning and end. The transportation requirement extends to all components and elements of the student's educational program, including those which are offered at times other than the normal school day and locations other than the school campus. *Brent v. San Diego Unified Sch. Dist.*, 25 IDELR 344 (S.D. Calif. 1996); *San Diego Unified Sch. Dist.*, 28 IDELR 244 (SEA CS 1998) In *Board of Education of the Roslyn Union Free School District*, 27 IDELR 1113 (SEA NY 1998), the review officer determined that the school was obligated to provide the student with transportation from an after-school program to his home.

The various factors to be considered when determining if transportation is required for a student to receive educational benefit are the child's age, the distance to be traveled, the nature of the route, access to private assistance, and availability of public assistance. *Malehorn v. Hill City Sch. Dist.*, 27 IDELR 144 (S.D. 1997)

Decisions about transportation are individualized determinations which must be made by the student's IEP team. Transportation arrangements must then be set forth in detail in the student's IEP. *Highland Local Sch. Dist.*, 26 IDELR 224 (SEA Ohio 1997)

Special Education

> Specially designed instruction, at no cost to parents, to meet the unique needs of a child with a disability, including (a) instruction conducted in the classroom, in the home, in hospitals and institutions, and (b) instruction in physical education. 20 U.S.C. 1401 (25).

Special education includes speech-language pathology services, or any other related service, if the service is considered special education rather than a related service under State standards, travel training, and vocational education.

At no cost means that all specially-designed instruction is provided without charge, but does not preclude incidental fees that are normally charged to nondisabled students or their parents as a part of the regular education program.

Physical education means the development of physical and motor fitness, fundamental motor skills and patterns, and skills in aquatics, dance, and individual and group games and sports (including intramural and lifetime sports). Physical education includes special education, adapted physical education, movement education, and motor development.

Specially-designed instruction means adapting, as appropriate to the needs of an eligible child, the content, methodology, or delivery of instruction to address the unique needs of the child that result from the child's disability; and to ensure access of the child to the general curriculum, so that he or she can meet the educational standards within the jurisdiction of the public agency that apply to all children.

Travel training means enabling students to develop an awareness of the environment in which they live and to learn the skills necessary to move effectively and safely from place to place within that environment (e.g., in school, in the home, at work, and in the community).

Vocational education means organized educational programs that are directly related to the preparation of individuals for paid or unpaid employment, or for additional preparation for a career requiring other than a baccalaureate or advanced degree. 34 C.F.R. 300.26

Stay Put

During the pendency of any (due process) proceedings . . . the child shall remain in the then-current educational placement of such child. 20 U.S.C. 1415 (j); 34 C.F.R. 300.514

Supplementary Aids and Services

Aids, services and other supports that are provided in regular education classes or education-related settings to enable children with disabilities to be educated with nondisabled children to the maximum extent appropriate. 34 C.F.R. 300.28; 20 U.S.C. 1401 (29)

Aids and services are modifications or supports to the regular education program. Examples include, but are not limited to, special reading materials, large print books, curriculum adaptations, calculators, special seating arrangements, modified homework assignments, testing arrangements, or one-to-one aides. Supplementary aids and services may enable the student to advance toward attaining his or her annual goals, be involved and progress in the general education curriculum, participate in extracurricular and other nonacademic activities, and be educated and participate in activities with other students with and without disabilities. All supplementary aids and services to be provided must be explicitly stated in the IEP.
Individual Educational Plans and IDEA 97, Technical Assistance Paper, Florida Department of Education, FY 1999-4D, August 1998.

Transition Services

"One must learn by doing the thing." Aristotle

A coordinated set of activities for a student with a disability that (a) is designed within an outcome-oriented process, that promotes movement from school to post-school activities, including postsecondary education, vocational training, integrated employment, (including supported employment) continuing and adult education,

Definitions

adult services, independent living, or community participation; (b) is based on the individual student's needs, taking into account the student's preferences and interests; and (c) includes instruction, related services, community experiences, the development of employment and other post-school adult living objectives; and, if appropriate, acquisition of daily living skills and functional vocational evaluation. 34 C.F.R. 300.29; 20 U.S.C. 1401 (30)

Transition services for students with disabilities may be special education, if provided as specially designed instruction, or related services, if required to assist a student with a disability to benefit from special education. 34 C.F.R. 300.29

Privilege

A handicap is an irrelevant
And needless thing,
But if you have your choice,
Get yourself one.

It teaches you some aloneness,
Some facts,
Some differences from other people
That you might fear at first
But love at last.

You have a chance to observe
From the outside
And to learn
How not to pity yourself–
A healthy lesson.

And eventually, through all
This growing,
You discover that everybody,
Being human
Is handicapped by the problem
Of learning to live wisely,

More properly called
The privilege of learning
To love wisely.

Charles B. Tinkham

Chapter 3

Identification

"The greatest gift we give others is helping them discover who they really are."

Unknown

Child Find

All children with disabilities residing in the State, including children with disabilities attending private schools, regardless of the severity of their disabilities, and who are in need of special education and related services, are identified, located, and evaluated and a practical method is developed and implemented to determine which

> **Noteworthy**
>
> The school has an obligation to find children who are suspected of having disabilities and in need of special education.

children with disabilities are currently receiving needed special education and related services. 20 U.S.C. 1412 (a) (3) (A); 34 C.F.R. 300.300 (a) (2)

Child find applies to highly mobile children with disabilities (such as migrant and homeless children) and children who are suspected of being children with disabilities and in need of special education, even though they are advancing from grade to grade. 34 C.F.R. 300.125 (a) (2)

Chapter 4

Evaluation

*"The noblest service comes from nameless hands,
and the best servant does his work unseen."*
                                    Oliver Wendall Holmes

Initial Evaluation

An evaluation consists of procedures used to determine whether a child has a disability and the nature and extent of the special education and related services that the child needs.34 C.F.R. 300.500 (b) (2)

An initial evaluation is the first completed assessment. The local educational agency shall conduct a full and individual initial evaluation before the initial provision of special education and related services to a child with a disability. In the case of an initial evaluation, a variety of assessment tools and strategies should be used to gather relevant functional and developmental information. These include information provided by the parent that may assist in determining whether the child is a child with a disability and the content of the child's individualized education program, including information related to enabling the child to be involved in and progress in the general curriculum. More than one procedure should be used as the criterion for determining whether a child is a child with a disability or determining an appropriate educational program for the child. 20 U.S.C. 1414 (b) (2) (A)

The tests and other evaluation materials used to assess a child must be selected and administered so as not to be discriminatory on a racial or cultural basis. The tests must be provided in the child's native language or other mode of communication unless it is not feasible to do so. Materials and procedures used to assess a child with limited English proficiency must be selected and administered to ensure that they measure the extent to which a child has a disability and needs special education, rather than measuring the child's English language skills. 34 C.F.R. 300.532

> **Noteworthy**
>
> No evaluations without parental consent.

If an assessment is not conducted under standard conditions, a description of the extent to which it varied from standard conditions (e.g., the qualifications of the person administering the test, or the method of test administration) must be included in the evaluation report. 34 C.F.R. 300.532

In evaluating each child with a disability under the procedures required by the Regulations (34 C.F.R. 300.531 through 34 C.F.R. 300.536), the evaluation should be sufficiently comprehensive to identify all of the child's special education and related services needs, whether or not commonly linked to the disability category in which the child is classified.

The results of the evaluation must be considered by the child's IEP team in developing the IEP. 34 C.F.R. 300.320 (b) (2)

The school must obtain an informed consent from the parent before an evaluation is conducted. However, parental consent is not required before administering a test used with all children. 34 C.F.R. 300.505 (a) (3) Parental consent for evaluation is not to be construed as consent for placement for receipt of special education and related services. If the parent refuses consent for the evaluation, the school may continue to pursue an evaluation by utilizing mediation and due process procedures. 20 U.S.C. 1414 (a) (1) (C)

Re-Evaluation

"Surrender to the fact that life isn't fair."
Richard Carlson

Once a child has been fully evaluated the first time, a decision has been rendered that a child is eligible under IDEA, and the required services have been determined, any subsequent evaluation of a child is considered a re-evaluation. A re-evaluation must be conducted if conditions warrant a re-evaluation or if the child's parent or teacher requests a re-evaluation, but at least once every three years. 20 U.S.C. 1414 (a) (2)

As a part of any re-evaluation, the IEP team and other qualified professionals, as appropriate, shall:

(1) review existing evaluation data on the child, including evaluation information provided by the parents of the child, current classroom-based assessments and observations, and teacher and related services providers observation; and

(2) on the basis of that review, and input from the child's parents, identify what additional data, if any, are needed to determine:

   (a) whether the child has a particular category of disability, or, in the case of a re-evaluation of a child, whether the child continues to have such a disability;

   (b) the present levels of performance and educational needs of the child;

   (c) whether the child needs special education and related services, or in the case of a re-evaluation of a child, whether the child continues to need special education and related services;

   (d) whether any additions or modifications to special education and related services are needed to enable the child to meet the measurable annual goals set out in the individualized education program of the child and to participate, as appropriate, in the general curriculum. 20 U.S.C. 1414 (c) (1)

Whether additional data is needed as part of the re-evaluation must be determined on a case-by-case basis, depending on the needs of the child and the information available regarding the child. The school must ensure that the group making the determination of the need for addi-

Evaluation

tional data includes individuals beyond the IEP team, if necessary, in order to made appropriate, informed decisions. If the IEP team and other qualified professionals, as appropriate, determine that no additional data are needed to determine whether the child continues to be a child with a disability, the school shall notify the child's parents of that determination and the reasons for it and the right of such parents to request an assessment to determine whether the child continues to be a child with a disability. This assessment shall not be required unless requested by the child's parents. 20 U.S.C. 1414 (c) (4)

Parental consent is required prior to conducting any re-evaluation, except that such informed consent need not be obtained if the school can demonstrate that it took reasonable measures to obtain such consent and the child's parent has failed to respond.

> *Noteworthy*
>
> Re-evaluation required if needed or requested, but at least every three years.

20 U.S.C. 1414 (c) (3) Reasonable measures are procedures consistent with those made in ensuring parental participation in IEP meetings, including telephone calls, correspondence and visits to the home. Parental consent is not required before reviewing existing data as part of an evaluation or a reevaluation. 34 C.F.R. 300.505

If the parent refuses to consent to a re-evaluation, due process or mediation is available for the school. 34 C.F.R. 300.505 (b) The results of any re-evaluation must be addressed by the child's IEP team in reviewing and, as appropriate, revising the child's IEP. 34 C.F.R. 300.321 (b)

The school shall re-evaluate before determining that a child is no longer a child with a disability. 20 U.S.C. 1414 (c) (5) Re-evaluation is not required, however, for graduation with a regular diploma or termination of eligibility for exceeding the age of eligibility. 34 C.F.R. 300.534 (c)

The school is entitled to conduct a three-year re-evaluation of a student even without the parents' consent because IDEA requires it. *Shasta Union H.S. Dist.*, 30 IDELR 733 (SEA CA 1999). The school will be given permission to conduct the evaluation despite the parents' objections if the evaluations are warranted. *Lewisville Independent Sch. Dist.*, 28 IDELR 1024 (SEA TX 1998) Moreover, the parents may be ordered to cooperate with the school's attempts to complete the re-evaluation. *Oregon City Sch. District 62*, 28 IDELR 536 (SEA ORE 1998)

Independent Educational Evaluation (IEE)

"Search for the grain of truth in others' opinions."
Richard Carlson

Independent evaluations are covered in the Procedural Safeguards sections of IDEA and the Regulations. An independent evaluation is an evaluation conducted by a qualified examiner who is not employed by the public agency. If a parent requests an independent evaluation at public expense, the school must, without unnecessary delay, either initiate a hearing to show that its evaluation is appropriate or ensure that an independent educational evaluation is provided at public expense. If the school initiates a hearing and the final decision is that the agency's evaluation is appropriate, the parent still has the right to an independent educational evaluation, but not at public expense. *San Antonio Independent Sch. Dist.*, 29 IDELR 630 (SEA TX 1998) Low scores do not invalidate an evaluation. *Long Beach Unified School Dist.*, 28 IDELR 777 (SEA CA 1998) If the student is evaluated by licensed and/or certified individuals and testing is conducted in all areas of suspected disability, the evaluation is appropriate. *Board of Educ. of the Victor Central Sch. Dist.*, 27 IDELR 1159 (SEA NY 1998)

> **Noteworthy**
>
> If parents request an IEE, school must grant it or go to due process to defend its evaluation.

If a parent requests an independent education evaluation, the school may ask for the parent's reason why he objects to the public evaluation. However, the explanation by the parent may not be required and the school may not unreasonably delay either providing the independent educational evaluation at public expense or initiating a due process hearing to defend the public evaluation.

If a parent refuses to consent to a proposed school evaluation in the first place, then an independent educational evaluation at public expense will not be available since there is no school evaluation with which the parent can disagree. Before a district is required to fund an IEE, the parents must object to the district's evaluation and the district's evaluation must be deemed inappropriate. *West Contra Costa Unified School District*, 28 IDELR 802 (SEA CA 1998)

The criteria under which the independent evaluation is

obtained must be the same as the criteria which the school used when it initiated the evaluation, but the criteria must be consistent with the parent's right to an independent educational evaluation. The school's criteria applicable to independent educational evaluations must be included as part of the information regarding independent educational evaluations provided, on request, to the parents.

The results of the independent evaluation must be considered by the IEP team in any decision made with respect to the provision of FAPE to the child. 34 C.F.R.300.502 (c) Failure to consider the results of an IEE when determining the appropriate placement for the student violates federal law and denies the student FAPE. *Community Consolidated School Dist. No. 180*, 27 IDELR 1004 (SEA Ill. 1998)

Chapter 5

Determination of Eligibility

"To understand and accept each other's differences, we must learn to listen with an open mind."
Unknown

Upon completing the administration of tests and other evaluation materials, a group of qualified professionals and the parent of the child determine whether the child is a child with a disability. The school provides a copy of the evaluation report and the documentation of determination of eligibility to the parent. Neither the statute nor the Regulations establish a timeline for providing these documents to the parents. However, parents and other IEP team participants must have all the infor-

> **Noteworthy**
>
> Parents must be involved in eligibility decisions.

mation they need to participate meaningfully in the IEP meeting.

A child will not be determined to be eligible if the determinant factor for that eligibility determination is lack of instruction in reading or math or limited English proficiency; and/or if the child does not otherwise meet the eligibility criteria.

> **Noteworthy**
>
> Parents are entitled to a copy of evaluations.

To have a determination of IDEA eligibility, a child must meet a two-part test. The child must be classified into one or more of the 13 categories of disability under IDEA and, as a result of that disability, the child must need special education and related services. A determination as to whether this criteria is met occurs through IDEA's evaluation process. *Letter to Anonymous,* 30 IDELR 538 (OSEP 1998)

The Sculptor

*I took a piece of plastic clay
And idly fashioned it one day,
And as my fingers pressed it, still
It bent and yielded to my will.*

*I came again, when days were passed,
The bit of clay was hard at last,
The form I gave it, still it bore,
But I could change that form no more.*

*Then I took a piece of living clay,
And gently formed it, day by day,
And molded with my power and art,
A young child's soft and yielding heart.*

*I came again when years were gone,
It was a man I looked upon.
He still that early impress bore,
And I could change it, nevermore.*

Unknown

Student Artist: Meagan Tarantelli
Pine Ridge Middle School, Naples, Florida
Teachers: Carol Mullen and Danielle Yarusevich

Chapter 6

Individualized Education Programs

"Through commitment and action, we effect much needed change."

Helen Caldicott

Overview

An IEP is a written statement for each child with a disability that is developed, reviewed, and revised by the IEP team. The IEP should be long enough to describe a child's program. However, the IEP is not intended to be a detailed instructional plan. An IEP is an "educational record" as that term is used in Family Educational Rights and Privacy Act and its Regulations (34 C.F.R. 99.3) and is, therefore, subject to the same protections as other educational records relating to the student.

The IEP has been described as "the basic mechanism through which the goal of providing FAPE is achieved for each disabled child." *O'Toole by O'Toole v. Olathe Dist. Schs. Unified Sch. Dist. No. 233,* 28 IDELR 177 (10th Cir., 1998)

At the beginning of each school year, the school shall have an IEP in effect for each child with a disability within its jurisdiction. Each school shall ensure that an IEP is in effect before special education and related services are provided to an eligible child and that it is implemented as soon as possible following the IEP meeting. C.F.R. 300.342 (a) (b) The school shall ensure that the child's IEP is accessible to each regular education teacher, special education teacher, related service provider, and other service providers responsible for its implementation. Each teacher and provider must be informed of his or her specific responsibilities related to implementing the child's IEP, as well as the specific accommodations, modifications, and supports that must be provided for the child in accordance with the IEP. 34 C.F.R. 300.342 (b) In developing each child's IEP, the IEP team must consider the strengths of the child, the results of evaluations, and the results of the child's performance on any general State or district-wide assessments. 34 C.F.R. 300.346 (a)

Content

"A powerful agent is the right word."
Mark Twain

An IEP includes:

> (1) *a statement of the child's present levels of educational performance,* including

(a) how the child's disability affects the child's involvement and progress in the general curriculum; or

(b) for preschool children, as appropriate, how the disability affects the child's participation in appropriate activities;

(2) *a statement of measurable annual goals including benchmarks or short-term objectives,* related to

(a) meeting the child's needs that result from the child's disability to enable the child to be involved in and progress in the general curriculum; and

(b) meeting each of the child's other educational needs that result from the child's disability. 34 C.F.R. 300.347 (a)

The revised IDEA and Regulations provide that, as an alternative, IEP teams may develop benchmarks, which can be thought of as describing the amount of progress the child is expected to make within specified segments of the year. Generally, benchmarks establish expected performance levels that allow for regular checks of progress than coincide with the reporting periods for informing parents of their child's progress toward achieving the annual goals. An IEP team may use either short term objectives or benchmarks or a combination of the two depending on the nature of the annual goals and the needs of the child. 34 C.F.R. Part 300, Appendix A

> ***Noteworthy***
>
> An incorrectly written IEP leads to litigation.

(3) *a statement of the special education and related services and supplementary aids and services to be provided to the child,* or on behalf of the child, and *a statement of the program modifications or supports* for school personnel that will be provided for the child

    (a) to advance appropriately toward attaining the annual goals. 34 C.F.R. 300.347 (a)

An IEP team is not required to include annual goals that relate to areas of the general curriculum in which the child's disability does not affect the child's ability to be involved in and progress in the general curriculum. If a child with a disability needs only modifications or accommodations in order to progress in an area of the general curriculum, the IEP does not need to include a goal for that area; the IEP would need to specify only those modifications and/or accommodations. 34 C.F.R. Part 300, Appendix A

    (b) to be involved and progress in the general curriculum and to participate in extracurricular and other nonacademic activities, and

    (c) to be educated and participate with other children with disabilities and non-disabled children in activities;

(4) *an explanation of the extent, if any, to which the child will not participate with nondisabled children* in the regular class and in activities;

    (a) a statement of any individual modifications in the administration of State or districtwide assessments of student achievement that are needed in order for the child to participate in such assessment;

(b) if the IEP Team determines that the child will not participate in a particular State or districtwide assessment of student achievement, a statement of why that assessment is not appropriate for the child; and how the child will be assessed;

(5) *the projected date for the beginning of the services and modifications, and the anticipated frequency, location, and duration of those services and modifications;*

(6) beginning at age 14, and updated annually, *a statement of the transitions service needs of the child* under the applicable components of the child's IEP that focuses on the child's courses of study;

beginning at age 16 (or younger if determined appropriate by the IEP Team), a statement of needed transition services for the child, including, when appropriate, a statement of the interagency responsibilities or any needed linkages;

and beginning at least one year before the child reaches the age of majority under State law, a statement that the child has been informed of his or her *rights,* if any, *that will transfer to the child* on reaching the age of majority. 34 C.F.R. 300.347 (a) (b)

A State may provide that, when a student with a disability reaches the age of majority under State law (unless determined to be incompetent), the school shall provide required notice to both the individual and the parents; and all other rights accorded to parents transfer to the student. 34 C.F.R.300.517

(7) a statement of
  (a) how the child's progress toward the annual goals will be measured; and
  (b) *how the child's parents will be regularly informed* at least as often as parents are informed of their nondisabled children's progress, of their child's progress toward the annual goals, and the extent to which that progress is sufficient to enable the child to achieve the goals by the end of the year. 34 C.F.R. 300.347 (a)

Participation in Assessments

> *"A mind, stretched to a new idea, never goes back to its original dimensions."*
>
> Oliver Wendall Holmes

A child with a disability must participate in State and local-wide assessments with accommodations where necessary. The test results must be reported with the same frequency and in the same detail as those on nondisabled children. Not later than July 1, 2000, the State must begin reporting the progress of disabled children on alternate assessments. 20 U.S.C. 1412 (a) (17)

> ### Noteworthy
>
> Remember that The Team has a right to have a copy of the IEP and anyone concerned with the child must have access to it.

The IEP Team

> *"Coming together is a beginning; keeping together is progress; working together is success."*
>
> Henry Ford

The school must ensure that all individuals who are necessary to develop an IEP that will meet the child's unique needs, and ensure the provision of FAPE to the child, participate in the child's IEP meeting. The IEP team is composed of

(1) The *parents* of the child with a disability (parent also includes a person "acting in the place of a parent"). 34 C.F.R. 300.344

> *"A person's wealth can be measured by his love of children."*
>
> Unknown

The parent shall be invited to participate in all placement and eligibility determinations and in IEP meetings. 20 U.S.C. 1414 (f); 20 U.S.C. 1415 (b) (1) In developing the IEP the team shall consider the concerns of the parents for enhancing the education of their child. 20 U.S.C. 1414 (d) (3) The parents, however, may not choose the specific teacher, the curriculum, the methodology or the school site. *Greenbush Sch. Committee v. Mr. And Mrs. K. ex. rel. JK,* 26 IDELR 200 (D. Me. 1996) The general rule is that methodology decisions are left up to school districts as long as the program provides the student with FAPE. *O'Toole by O'Toole v. Olathe District Sch. Unified Sch. Dist. No 223,* 28 IDELR 177 (10th Cir. 1998)

The school shall take steps to ensure that the parents of a child with a disability are present at each IEP meeting or are afforded the opportunity to participate, including notifying parents of the meeting early enough to ensure that they will have an opportunity to attend; and scheduling the meeting at a mutually agreed on time and place. If neither parent can participate in a meeting in which a decision is to be made relating to the educational placement of the child, the school shall use other methods to ensure the parents' participation, including individual or conference telephone calls, or video conferencing. 34 C.F.R. 300.501 (b) (3) A meeting may be conducted without parents in attendance if the school is unable to convince the parents that they should attend. In that case the school must have a record of its attempts to arrange a mutually agreed on time and place, such as detailed records of telephone calls made or attempted and the results of those calls; copies of correspondence sent to the parents and any responses received; and detailed records of visits made to the parent's home or place of employment and the results of those visits. 34 C.F.R. 300.345 (a) (c) (d)

> ***Noteworthy***
>
> Be sure you have all the "players" at the IEP table.

The school erred when parents were excluded from participating in proceedings where the child's initial eligibility for special education was determined, and the form notice the parents received regarding an IEP meeting was deficient as it did not enable the parents to determine either the name or the position of the personnel who would be attending. Morever, the parents were not provided with a complete copy of the IEP, which the Court determined interfered with their meaningful participation in the IEP process. *Gwinnett Country School System,* 4 ECLPR, Sec. 98 (SEA Ga., 1999)

The Court invalidated an IEP when the school failed to provide the parents with the required notice of who would attend the meeting, when they failed to inform the parents of the purpose of the meeting, and when they presented the parents with a prepared IEP for the purpose of obtaining the parent's approval. The parents were never given a chance to make suggestions about the IEP or the placement it suggested. *Amanda S. by Susan S. v. Webster City Community School District,* 27 IDELR 698 (N.D. Iowa 1998).

The school erred when the parent was notified that a meeting would be held to "develop or review" the student's IEP, but was not informed that the primary topic for discussion was the proposed change in the student's placement. *Three Rivers/Josephine County School District,* 28 IDELR 1228, (SEA OR 1998)

Parents must be given a copy of the IEP without cost and without having to request it. C.F.R. 34 300.345 (f) In addition, the Regulations include parent counseling and training, as a related service. Parent counseling and training is defined as "helping parents to acquire the necessary skills that will allow them to support the implementation of their child's IEP". 34 C.F.R. 300.24 (7)

> (2) At least one *regular education teacher* of the child (if the child is, or may be, participating in the regular education environment). 34 C.F.R. 300.344

> *"A teacher affects eternity; she can never tell where her influence stops."*
>
> Henry B. Adams

The regular education teacher who serves as a member of a child's IEP team should be a teacher who is, or may be, responsible for implementing a portion of the IEP, so that the teacher can participate in discussions about the best methods to teach the child. If the child has more than one regular education teacher responsible for carrying out a portion of the IEP, the school may designate which teacher or teachers will serve as IEP team member(s), taking into account the best interest of the child. In a situation in which not all of the child's regular education teachers are members of the child's IEP team, input should be sought from the teachers who will not be attending. 34 C.F.R. Part 300, Appendix A, Question 26.

The regular education teacher of a child with a disability, as a member of the IEP team, must, to the extent appropriate, participate in the development, review, and revision of the child's IEP, including assisting in the determination of appropriate positive behavioral interventions and strategies, supplementary aids and services, and program modifications or supports that will be provided for the child to ensure the child's involvement and progress in the general curriculum and participation in the regular education environment. 34 C.F.R. 300.346 (d)

Under IDEA, the participation of at least one regular education teacher on the IEP team is mandated and cannot be excused. *Searcy Public Schools*, 30 IDELR 825 (SEA AR 1999) However, the teacher need not be required to partici-

Individualized Education Programs

pate in all decisions, to be present throughout the entire meeting, or to attend every meeting if the teacher is not responsible for implementing that portion of the child's IEP.

In determining the extent of the regular education teacher's participation at IEP meetings, schools and parents should discuss and try to reach agreement on whether the child's regular education teacher that is a member of the IEP team should be present at a particular IEP meeting and, if so, for what period of time. The extent to which it would be appropriate for the regular education teacher member of the IEP team to participate in IEP meetings must be decided on a case-by-case basis. 34 C.F.R. Part 300, Appendix A, Question 24

> ***Noteworthy***
>
> An IEP must be in effect for each child with a disability at the beginning of the school year and before special education services are provided.

> (3) At least one *special education teacher,* or where appropriate, at least one special education provider of such child. Another special education provider such as a speech-language pathologist, physical or occupational therapist, etc., should attend if the related service consists of specially designed instruction and is considered special education.
>
> (4) A representative of the *local educational agency* who is qualified to provide, or supervise the provision of, specially designed instruction to meet the unique

needs of children with disabilities; is knowledgeable about the general curriculum; and is knowledgeable about the availability of resources of the local educational agency. 34 C.F.R. 300.344

As long as a person meets the criteria, listed in paragraph (4) above, that person can be the LEA representative at the IEP meeting. For example, if a school psychologist or guidance counselor meets those criteria, he/she could serve as the LEA representative. *Letter to Collins,* 30 IDELR 404 (OSEP, 1998)

> (5) An *individual who can interpret the instructional implications of evaluation results,* who may already be a member of the team.
>
> (6) At the discretion of the parent or the school, *other individuals* who have knowledge or special expertise regarding the child, including related services personnel as appropriate. 34 C.F.R. 300.344

No limitation on the number of individuals who can attend IEP meetings should be imposed. The determination of the knowledge or special expertise of any individual brought by the parent or the school shall be made by the party who invited the individual to be a member of the IEP team. 34 C.F.R. 300.344 (c) It is appropriate to ask the parents to inform the school of any individual the parents will be bringing to the meeting. Such cooperation can facilitate arrangements for the meeting and help to ensure a productive, child-centered meeting. 34 C.F.R. Part 300, Appendix A

Where no representatives of the proposed placements were present at an IEP meeting and no one else could provide this information, parents were not fully informed about those placement options. *McMillan by Collins v. Cheatham County Schools,* 25 IDELR 398 (M.D. Tenn. 1997)

> (7) Whenever appropriate, the **child** with a disability. 34 C.F.R. 300.344

The school shall invite a student with a disability of any age to attend his or her IEP meeting if the purpose of the meeting is to consider the student's transition needs. If the student does not attend the IEP meeting, the school shall take other steps to ensure that the student's preferences and interests are considered. 34 C.F.R. 300.344 (b)

Review and Revision of the IEP

> *"An enthusiastic team of talented individuals knows no boundaries."*
>
> Unknown

The IEP team shall review the child's IEP periodically, but not less than annually, to determine whether the annual goals for the child are being achieved; and revise the IEP as appropriate to address:

> (1) Any lack of expected progress toward the annual goals and in the general curriculum, where appropriate;
>
> (2) The results of any reevaluation;

(3) Information about the child provided to, or by, the parents;

(4) The child's anticipated needs, or

(5) Other matters. 34 C.F.R. 300.343 (c)

Although the school is responsible for determining when it is necessary to conduct an IEP meeting, the parents of a child with a disability have the right to request an IEP meeting at any time. *Letter to Slatkin,* 213:128, OSERS 1998 Schools should grant any reasonable parent requests for an IEP meeting. If a parent requests an IEP meeting because the parent believes that a change is needed in the provision of FAPE to the child or the educational placement of the child, and the school refuses to convene an IEP meeting to determine whether such a change is needed, the school must provide written notice to the parents of the refusal, including an explanation of why the school has determined that conducting the meeting is not necessary to ensure the provision of FAPE to the student. 34 C.F.R., Part 300, Appendix A, Question 20

IEP Meetings

"We are continually faced by great opportunities brilliantly disguised as insolvable problems."
Unknown

Consensus

The IEP team should work toward consensus, but the school has the ultimate responsibility to ensure that the IEP includes the services that the child needs to receive FAPE. It is not appropriate to make IEP decisions based upon a majority "vote". If the team cannot reach consensus, the school must provide the parents with prior written notice of the school's proposals or refusals, or both, regarding the child's educational program, and the parents have the right to seek resolution of any disagreements by initiating an impartial due process hearing. 34 C.F.R. Part 300, Appendix A.

What Is NOT an IEP Meeting?

"The courage to speak must be matched by the wisdom to listen."

Unknown

An IEP meeting does not include informal or unscheduled conversations involving school personnel and conversations on issues such as teaching methodology, lesson plans, or coordination of service provision if those issues are not addressed in the child's IEP. A meeting also does not include preparation activities by school personnel to develop a proposal or respond to a parent proposal that will be discussed at a later meeting. 34 C.F.R 300.501 (b) (2) A visit to a classroom is generally not a meeting. *Letter to Blades,* 213:169, OSERS, 1988. Reviewing data to determine the extent of re-evaluation necessary may also be done without convening an IEP meeting. 34 C.F.R. 300.533

> **Noteworthy**
>
> An IEP team works toward consensus.

49

Informal discussions among teachers and administrators, which may or may not be prearranged, are not meetings for which parents must receive notice and the opportunity to attend. Whether or not a meeting is prearranged is not the deciding factor in determining whether parents would have the right to attend. Rather, what triggers the parents' right to be involved is if the purpose of the meeting is to discuss and potentially resolve issues related to the identification, evaluation, and educational placement, and the provision of FAPE to the child. *Letter to Blades,* 213:169, OSERS, 1988

Recording Devices

IDEA does not address the use of audio or video recording devices at IEP meetings, and no other Federal statute either authorizes or prohibits the recording of an IEP meeting by either a parent or a school official. Therefore, a state or school district has the option to require, prohibit, limit, or otherwise regulate the use of recording devices at an IEP meeting. If a school district has a policy that prohibits or limits the use of recording devices at IEP meetings, that policy must provide for exceptions if they are necessary to ensure that the parent understands the IEP or the IEP process or to implement other parental rights guaranteed under IDEA. Any recording of an IEP meeting that is maintained by the school is an educational record, within the meaning of the Family Educational Rights and Privacy Act (20 U.S.C. 1232 g) and would, therefore, be subject to the confidentiality requirements of that Act. 34 C.F.R. Part 300, Appendix A

Accountability

> *"In all human affairs, there are efforts and there are results, and the strength of the effort is the measure of the result."*
>
> James Lane Allen

Each school must provide special education and related services to a child with a disability in accordance with the child's IEP and make a good faith effort to assist the child to achieve the goals and objectives or benchmarks listed in the IEP. The law does not require that any school district, teacher, or other person be held accountable if a child does not achieve the growth projected in the annual goals and benchmarks or objectives. However, a parent has the right to ask for revisions of the IEP or to invoke due process procedures if the parent feels that good faith efforts are not being utilized. 34 C.F.R. 300 (b) (c)

> **Noteworthy**
>
> A child with a disability is entitled to an "IEP report card."

Under IDEA, the school is not required to use a specific term to describe a student's disability in creating an IEP. Moreover, the school is only required to provide the student with a "basic floor of opportunity." *Cronkite v. Long Beach Unified Sch. Dist.*, 30 IDELR 510 (9th Cir., 1999) The "appropriate" education required by IDEA is not one which is guaranteed to maximize the child's potential. The "best possible education" is not required, nor are "superior results" promised. *O'Toole by O'Toole v. Olathe Dist. Schs. Uni-*

fied Sch. Dist. No. 233, 28 IDELR 177 (10th Cir., 1998) An IEP must be likely to produce progress, not regression or trivial educational advancement. In short, the educational benefit that an IEP is designed to achieve must be "meaningful." *Tucson Unified Sch. Dist.,* 30 IDELR 478 (SEA Ariz. 1999)

The IEP must include a statement of how the child's progress toward the annual goals or benchmarks will be measured and how the child's parents will be regularly informed at least as often as parents of nondisabled children are informed of their progress. These reports to parents are intended to be in addition to, not in the place of, the district's regular reports to parents of all children. 20 U.S.C. 1414 (d) (1) (A); 34 C.F.R. 300.347

Since the IEP is a program, consisting of both the written IEP document, and the subsequent implementation of that document, courts will evaluate the IEP as an on-going, dynamic activity. A school cannot ignore the fact that an IEP is clearly failing, nor can it continue to implement year after year, without change, an IEP which fails to confer educational benefits on the student. *O'Toole by O'Toole v. Olathe Dist. Schs. Unified Sch. Dist. No. 233,* 28 IDELR 177 (10th Cir., 1998)

A school violated FAPE by failing to properly advise the parent of the child's progress and what would be necessary for the child to succeed in school. *Tuscaloosa County School Board,* 30 IDELR 842 (SEA AL 1999)

Heaven's Special Child

A meeting was held quite far from earth
  "It's time for another birth,"
Said the angels of the Lord above.
  This special child will need much love,

His progress may seem rather slow,
  And some accomplishments he may not show.
He may even require some extra care
  From all the folks he meets down there.

He may not see, or hear, or run or play;
  His thoughts might even seem far away.
In some ways he may not be able to adapt,
  Some may even call him handicapped.

So let's be careful where he's sent,
  We certainly want his life to be content.
Lord, find the parents and teachers who
  Can do this very special job for you.
They may not realize right away,
  The leading role they're asked to play,
But with this special child from above,
  Will come stronger faith and richer love.

And soon they will know the privilege given
  In caring for this special gift from heaven.
This precious child, sometimes difficult,
  Sometimes mild
Is surely Heaven's Special Child.

Author Unknown

Kids Who Are Different

Here's to the kids who are different,
 The kids who don't always get A's,
The kids who have ears twice the size of their peers,
 And noses that go on for days...

Here's to the kids who are different,
 The kids they call crazy or dumb,
The kids who don't fit, with the guts and the grit,
 Who dance to a different drum...

Here's to the kids who are different,
 The kids with the mischievous streak,
For when they have grown, as history's shown,
 It's their difference that makes them unique.

Copyright 1982 by Digby Wolfe, All rights reserved.

Chapter 7

Placement

"We cannot direct the wind, but we can adjust the sails."

Unknown

In determining the educational placement of a child with a disability, including a preschool child with a disability, each school shall ensure that the placement decision is made by a group of persons, including the parents, and other persons knowledgeable about the child, the meaning of the evaluation data, and the placement options. The school shall make reasonable efforts to ensure that the parents understand, and are able to participate in, any group discussion relating to the educational placement of their child, including arranging for

> ***Noteworthy***
>
> Placement decisions are made by IEP teams.

an interpreter for parents with deafness, or whose native language is other than English. 34 C.F.R. 300.501(c)

The IEP forms the basis for the placement decision. 34 C.F.R. Part 300, Appendix A It is a violation of IDEA to change a student's placement without including the entire IEP team in the placement decision. *Dallas School District*, 28 IDELR 1225 (SEA TX 1998)

A change in location, without a change in the special education services to be provided, does not result in a change of placement. *Morris by Morris v. Metropolitan Gov't of Nashville and Davidson County*, 26 IDELR 159 (M.D. Tenn. 1997)

> **Noteworthy**
>
> Regular education is always the first placement option, but placement decisions are made individually.

The school must also ensure that the child's placement is determined at least annually, is based on the child's IEP, and is as close as possible to the child's home. Unless the IEP of a child with a disability requires some other arrangement, the child must be educated in the school that he or she would attend if nondisabled. A child may not be removed from education in age-appropriate regular classrooms solely because of needed modifications in the general curriculum. 34 C.F.R. 300.552 This is consistent with the least restrictive environment provisions of the Regulations which provide that each child with a disability be educated with nondisabled children to the maximum extent appropriate and that each child with a disability be removed from the regular educational environment only when the nature or severity of the child's disability is such that education in regular classes with the use of supplementary aids and services cannot be achieved satisfactorily. 34 C.F.R. 300.550 (b) (l)

Federal courts have developed a four-prong test in evaluating the appropriateness of a placement in the least restrictive environment:

1. What are the educational benefits to the student in the general education classroom, with supplementary aids and service, as compared to the educational benefits of a special education classroom?
2. What will be the non-academic or personal benefits to the student in interactions with peers who do not have disabilities?
3. What would be the effect of the presence of the student on the teacher and other students in the general education classroom?
4. What would be the relative costs for providing necessary supplementary aids and services to the student in the general education classroom?

Oberti v. Clemson Sch. Dist., 995 F. 2d 1204 (3rd Cir., 1993), 19 IDELR 908

Even though IDEA does not mandate regular class placement for every disabled student, IDEA presumes that the first placement option considered for each disabled student by the IEP team is the school the child would attend if not disabled, with appropriate supplementary aids and services to facilitate such placement. Regular education is always the first placement considered, but in all cases, placement decisions must be individually determined on the basis of each child's abilities and needs. *Letter to Hale,* 30 IDELR 142 (OSEP, 1997) Placement cannot be made solely on factors such as category of disability, significance of disability, availability of special education and related services, configuration of the service delivery system, availability of space, or administrative convenience.

> **Noteworthy**
>
> Each school shall ensure that a continuum of placements is available.

Each school shall ensure that a continuum of alternative placements is available to meet the needs of children with disabilities for special education and related services. The continuum must include instruction in regular classes, special classes, special schools, home instruction, and instruction in hospitals and institutions and must make provision for supplementary services to be provided in conjunction with regular class placement. 20 U.S.C. 1412 (a) (5); 34 C.F.R. 300.551

Chapter 8

Discipline of a Student with a Disability

"Make the work interesting and the discipline will take care of itself."

E. B. White

Many changes were made in the 1999 Regulations as a result of the concerns of school administrators and teachers regarding school safety and order. Significant is the fact that a child with a disability who is experiencing significant disciplinary problems may be removed to another placement. A change of placement occurs if the removal is for more than 10 consecutive school days or if the child is subjected to a series of removals that cumulate to more than 10 school days in a school year, and constitute a pattern because of the length of each removal, the total amount of time the child is removed, and/or the proximity of the removals to one another. 34 C.F.R. 300.519 The Regulations do not enumerate any hard-and-fast rules for discerning what constitutes a "pattern of removals." Whether a pattern of removals constitutes a change in placement is determined on a case-by-case basis and is subject to review through due process and judicial proceedings.

A school cannot refer to a removal as a "short-term suspension" when it really amounts to an indefinite removal. *Sherry v. New York State Educ. Dept.* 479 F. Supp. 1328 (W.D.N.Y. 1979). If bus suspension results in failure to implement an IEP, it counts toward the 10-day count of change of placement. *Buncombe County Sch. Dist.,* 23 IDELR 364 (OCR 1995)

> **Noteworthy**
>
> Change of placement means removal from school for more than 10 consecutive days or a series of removals that cumulate to more than 10 days.

After a child with a disability has been removed from his current placement for more than 10 school days in the same school year, the school must provide services during any subsequent days of removal. 34 C.F.R. 300.520 (a) (l) (ii) Services do not have to be provided in situations where a student has been removed for 10 school days or less in a school year, if services would normally not be provided to a similarly-situated non disabled student. 34 C.F.R. 300.121 (d) (1)

Any time a child's placement is changed, an IEP meeting must be held. *District of Columbia Public Schools.* 28 IDELR 401 (SEA D.C. 1998)

Because a long-term suspension is a change in placement, schools must give the parents prior written notice. 34 C.F.R. 300.503 (a)

> The written notice to parents must include, among other matters, the determination that the student's misconduct was not a manifestation of the student's disability and the basis for that determination, and an explanation of applicable procedural safeguards, including the right of the student's parents to initiate an impartial due process hearing to challenge the manifestation determination and to seek administrative or judicial review of an adverse decision. OSEP Memorandum 95-16, 22 IDELR 531, 1995

Placement in an Alternative Educational Setting

> *"The significant problems we face cannot be solved at the same level of thinking we were at when we created them."*
> — Albert Einstein

School personnel may order a change in the placement of a child with a disability (a) to an appropriate interim alternative educational setting, another setting, or suspension, for not more than 10 school days (to the extent such alternatives would be applied to children without disabilities); and (b) to an appropriate interim alternative educational setting for the same amount of time that a child without a disability would be subject to discipline, but not more than 45 days if (l) the child carries or possesses a weapon to or at school, on school premises, or to a school function under the jurisdiction of a State or a local educational agency; or (2) the child knowingly possesses or uses illegal drugs or sells or solicits the sale of a controlled substance while at school or a school function. U.S.C. 20 1415 (k) (1) (A)

Note that the statutory phrase "carries a weapon to school or to a school function" also includes situations where a student acquires a weapon at school. The amended statute went into effect at the start of the 1999-2000 school year.

A hearing officer may order placement in an interim alternative educational setting for not more than 45 days if the hearing officer, in an expedited due process hearing:

(1) Determines that the school had demonstrated by substantial evidence that maintaining the current placement of the child is substantially likely to result in injury to the child or others. 34 C.F.R. 300.521 (a)

"Substantial evidence" is a greater quantum of evidence than a litigant would need to prevail in a civil case, but less than the criminal standard of "beyond a reasonable doubt." It means beyond a preponderance of the evidence. 20 U.S.C. 1415 (k) (10) (C) The school must prove that the student is "dangerous." *Pottstown School Dist.*, 30 IDELR 651 (SEA PA 1999)

(2) Considers the appropriateness of the child's current placement. 34 C.F.R. 300.521 (b)

(3) Considers whether the school has made reasonable efforts to minimize the risk of harm in the child's current placement, including the use of supplementary aids and services. 34 C.F.R. 300.521 (c)

(4) Determines that the interim alternative educational setting proposed by school personnel who have consulted with the child's special education teacher, meets the requirements of Section 300.522 (Be selected so as to enable the child to continue to progress in the general curriculum, although in another setting, and to continue to receive those services and modifications, including those described in the child's current IEP, that will enable the child to meet the goals set out in that IEP; and include services and modifications to address the behavior described that are designed to prevent the behavior from recurring). 34 C.F.R. 300.521 (d)

A placement ordered pursuant to this regulation may not be longer than 45 days and the procedure in this section may be repeated. 34 C.F.R. 300.526 (c)

Unlike placement of a student who poses a danger to himself, or others, placement of a student for a drug or weapons offense cannot be extended or renewed. *Letter to Bachman,* 29 IDELR 1092 (OSEP, 1997)

If a student engages in separate instances of prohibited misconduct or dangerous behavior, he may be placed in an interim alternative educational placement on each occasion. The Department of Education stated:

> These Regulations do not prohibit a child with a disability from being subjected to a disciplinary suspension, including more than one placement in a 45-day interim alternative educational setting in any given school year, if that is necessary in an individual case. 64 Fed. Reg. 12648 (1999)

Neither the IDEA nor the Regulations explicitly allow a school district to seek a court injunction to remove a dangerous student from school. However, both the Office of Special Education Programs (OSEP) and recent court decisions are of the opinion that Congress did not intend to restrict a school's flexibility in dealing with dangerous students. The *Honig v. Doe* case (EHLR 559:231 (1988)), established the precedent that school districts may not, in the ordinary course, unilaterally remove behaviorally disordered students; instead, they must go to court and obtain an injunction. In its first guidance on the disciplinary provisions of IDEA, the Office of Special Education Programs stated that the statute does not bar school districts from seeking Honig court-ordered injunctions for removals of students. OSEP *Memorandum,* 26 IDELR 981, 983 (1997)

The Court for the Northern District of Alabama came to the same conclusion in 1998 when it rejected an interpretation of the new law under which a district must exhaust its administrative remedies under the Regulations before bringing an action in court seeking a Honig injunction. *Gadsden City Board of Education v. B. P.,* 28 IDELR 166 (N.D. Ala. 1998)

The alternative educational setting shall be determined

by the IEP team; school administrators are not authorized to assign a disabled student to an alternative educational setting. *Independent School Dist No. 279, Osseo Area School,* 30 IDELR 645 (SEA MN 1999)

If the IEP team properly determines that the behavior was not related to disability and complies with applicable procedural requirements (functional behavioral assessment, notice to parents, continuation of services), a student can be subjected to long-term disciplinary removals to the same extent as a similarly-situated non-disabled student. 20 U.S.C. 1415 (k)

Stay-put is not a procedural safeguard extended to a student with a disability who has been placed in an interim alternative educational placement. 34 C.F.R. 300.526; 20 U.S.C. 1415 (k) However, failure to comply with the procedural requirements may result in the student being entitled to remain in current educational setting during the pendency of a due process hearing. *William S. Hart Union High School Dist.,* 26 IDELR 1258 (SEA Calif., 1997)

> **Noteworthy**
>
> Special education students removed from school for more than 10 days are entitled to services.

If the student is clearly a danger to himself and others, the school may be given permission to place the student in a interim placement during the course of due process hearings instead of maintaining his current placement pursuant to the stay-put rule. *Community Consolidated School District 15,* 30 IDELR 448, (SEA IL, 1999)

The quality of educational services provided in an alternative educational setting has become an important issue in some of the first legal challenges to alternative educational placements. A New York review officer found that an alternative placement consisting of home instruction was inappropriate because it failed to provide any special education services that were in the students's IEP. *Bd. of Educ. Of the Akron Central School Dist.*, 28 IDELR 909 (SEA NY 1998). A Maine hearing officer found that an interim alternative educational setting that did not enable a student to continue to receive necessary services and modifications, including those needed to address the student's behavioral problems, was only partially appropriate. *Freeport Public Schools,* 26 IDELR 1251 (SEA ME 1997)

> **Noteworthy**
>
> Services may be provided in an alternative educational setting.

An Oregon hearing officer found that an alternative educational setting program that failed to include many IEP components previously provided to the student was inappropriate to meet a student's complex emotional and behavioral needs. The hearing officer stated: "The IDEA requires a district to demonstrate that the proposed interim placement is appropriate in that it allows the student to participate in the general curriculum, allows the student to meet the goals of the IEP and includes services and modifications to address the behavior which triggered the removal." *Oregon City School Dist.*, 28 IDELR 96 (SEA OR 1998)

A student was not allowed to be removed to an interim alternative educational placement when the school failed to provide any evidence that an interim alternative educational placement would provide the student with services and modifications required by his IEP and that the student would continue to progress in the general curriculum. *Pottstown School District,* 30 **IDELR** 651 (SEA PA 1999)

Functional Behavioral Assessment

"Look beyond the behavior."
Richard Carlson

> IEP teams are required to address a child's behavior through functional behavioral assessments and behavioral intervention plans within 10 business days of a child's removal for more than 10 school days in a school year, and, whenever the child is subjected to a disciplinary change of placement. 20 U.S.C. 1415 (k) (1)

IDEA did not define the term "functional behavioral assessment", but the law does provide that the school shall "use a variety of assessment tools and strategies to gather relevant functional and developmental information". 20 U.S.C. 1414 (b) (2) (A) Further, **IDEA** requires the use of "technically sound instruments that may assess the relative contribution of cognitive and behavioral factors . . . and assessment tools and strategies". 20 U.S.C. 1414 (b) (2) (C)

> The general purpose of functional assessment of behavior is to provide the IEP team with additional information, analysis, and strategies for dealing with undesirable behavior, especially when it is interfering with a child's

education. The process involves some variant of identifying the core or "target" behavior; observing the pupil (perhaps in different environments) and collecting data on the target behavior, antecedents, and consequences; formulating a hypothesis about the causes of the behavior; developing an intervention to test the hypothesis; and collecting data on the effectiveness of the intervention in changing the behavior. Presentation of the information should be done in a manner useful for future work on the child's behavioral issues. *Independent School District No. 2310,* 29 IDELR 330 (SEA Minn. 1998)

A functional behavioral assessment has been defined as "a process which searches for an explanation of the purpose behind a problem behavior." *Comments to Notice of Proposed Rulemaking,* 64 Fed. Reg. 12620 (1999)

A functional behavioral assessment has also been defined as "a process for developing a useful understanding of how behavior relates to the environment." The more severe the behavior and complex the circumstances, the greater will be the degree of precision and thoroughness that is required in the assessment process. By knowing the function (or purpose) that the behavior serves for the student, one is able to develop an intervention that also serves those functions, but does so through positive student behaviors.*

Functional assessment procedures typically include the following activities:

---

*Functional Behavioral Assessment and Behavioral Intervention Plans, Technical Assistance Paper, Florida Department of Education, FY 1999-3D, June 1998.

(1) observations of the behavior in one or more settings and at various times;

(2) interviews with individuals familiar with the student, such as family and teachers as well as the student in question;

(3) review of records including prior interventions and results; formal and informal measurement procedures.*

School personnel that can be utilized to conduct the functional behavioral assessments include certified behavioral specialists, school psychologists, guidance counselors, school social workers, exceptional education teachers, program specialists, and other personnel with specific training in behavior analysis and therapy.

Failure to comply with the requirement for functional behavioral assessments has been the subject of litigation since the Reauthorized IDEA was passed. In the case of *William S. Hart Union High Sch. Dist.*, 26 IDELR 1258 (SEA CA 1997), the district's failure to conduct a functional behavioral assessment, along with other violations, led the hearing officer to overturn an IEP placement for a student found smoking marihuana. Likewise, a New York hearing officer reversed an IEP placement for a student caught purchasing marihuana at school, because, along with other omissions, the district had "failed to properly develop an assessment plan to address the behavior which had been the

---

*Addressing Student Problem Behavior: An IEP Team's Introduction to Functional Behavioral Assessment and Behavior Intervention Plans, Center for Effective Collaboration and Practice , Washington, D.C. (1997)

subject of the discipline hearing." *Bd. of Educ. Of the Akron Central Sch. Dist,* 28 IDELR 909 (SEA NY 1998).

The school violated IDEA when the functional behavioral assessment conducted was seriously deficient and never completed. The hearing officer ruled that the school's failure resulted in a loss of educational benefit to the student. *Independent School Dist. No. 2310,* 29 IDELR 330 (SEA MN 1998)

Behavior Intervention Plans

> *"You have not converted a (child) because you have silenced him."*
>
> John Morley

> The IEP team is to consider, if appropriate, in the case of a child whose behavior impedes his or her learning or that of others, strategies, including positive behavioral interventions, strategies, and supports to address that behavior. 34 C.F.R. 300.346 (a) (2)

As soon as practicable after developing a behavior intervention plan and completing the assessments required by the plan, the school should convene an IEP meeting to develop appropriate behavioral interventions to address the behavior and to implement interventions. If subsequently a child with a disability who has a behavioral intervention plan and who has been removed from his current educational placement for more than 10 school days in a school year is subjected to a removal that does not constitute a change of placement, the IEP team members should review the behavioral intervention plan and its implementation to determine if modifications are necessary. If one or more of the team members believe that modifications are needed, the team shall meet to modify the plan and its implementation, to the extent the team determines necessary. 34 C.F.R. 300.520; (c) (l) (2)

The 1997 IDEA Amendments added the term "behavioral intervention plan", without a specific definition. In the absence of specificity in the federal law, a good starting point for understanding a behavioral intervention plan is the definition proposed by the National Association of Social Workers:

> ***Noteworthy***
> Functional behavioral assessments and behavioral intervention plans must be provided.

> A behavioral intervention plan can be generally defined as a written, specific, purposeful and organized plan which describes positive behavioral interventions and other strategies that will be implemented to address goals for a student's social, emotional and behavioral development within the context of the IEP process. In addition, for students whose behavior prompts disciplinary action by the school, the behavioral intervention plan address the behaviors of concern that led to conducting a functional behavioral analysis.*

In developing a behavioral intervention plan, the following are important points to remember:

---

*Accessed at the website of the National Association of Social Workers at www.maswdc.org/sections/SSW/schclark.htm

(1) The parent and student should be included in the development and implementation of the plan.

(2) The plan needs to be practical, workable, and reasonable for implementation in the targeted settings.

(3) Individuals responsible for carrying out the intervention plan should have the appropriate training and possess the required skills for successful plan implementation.

(4) The specifics of the intervention strategies should be identified, including time and duration, setting, and individual roles and responsibilities.

(5) There should be "buy-in" from the persons who will implement the plan and, where appropriate, acceptance of the plan by the student.

(6) Interventions that are considered should use the following approaches:

(a) adjust environment to prevent problems and promote positive behaviors;

(b) teach skills to a high level of competency (often referred to as replacement behaviors) that allow the student to achieve the same results as the problem behavior;

(c) manage consequences so that reinforcement is maximized for positive behaviors and minimized for problem behaviors.

(7) Well-designed classwide interventions may be very appropriate for some students; however, other children may required well-crafted, individualized interventions.

(8) Determine what is reinforcing to the individual child and create an appropriate reinforcement schedule for the situation. What is reinforcing to one may not be reinforcing to another. If at all possible, use the reinforcer that maintained the problem behaviors to reinforce the desired, replacement behaviors. For example, if a child sought attention through misbehavior, use attention to reinforce appropriate behavior.

(9) If consequences are used for problem behaviors, they must be immediate and consistent and not inadvertently reinforce the misbehavior. For instance, when a child seeks to escape an assignment by throwing workpapers on the floor, referrals to the office have a high probability of strengthening the misbehavior. It may be more effective for the teacher to offer the student the chance to complete part of the assignment followed by a short break.

(10) The application of highly restrictive, behavior change procedures should be done with caution and under the supervision of qualified behavior specialists.

(11) The intervention should be implemented consistently and for a reasonable duration in relevant school situations and in the home and community as appropriate.

(12) In some instances (when using selected behavior reduction techniques), an initial escalation of the behaviors targeted for elimination may occur.

(13) A procedure for objectively evaluating the effectiveness of the intervention on the targeted behaviors should be developed by the IEP team. It should

include the establishment of short and long-term goals, monitoring activities, and timelines for periodic review of intervention outcomes.

Functional behavioral assessments and behavioral intervention plans, although new under IDEA 1997, have already generated litigation. In the case of *Freeport Public Schools*, 26 IDELR 1251 (SEA ME 1997), the hearing officer overturned an IEP placement for a student who had brandished a knife at school, partly due to the district's failure to effectively utilize an evaluation to develop a behavior plan to address the student's anger control and aggression.

> **Noteworthy**
>
> If a child is subject to a disciplinary change of placement, a manifestation determination review is required.

In *Devine Independent School District*, 25 IDELR 1238 (SEA Tex. 1997), a hearing officer ruled that a student with a disability required an individual discipline plan in order to receive FAPE. A school district that did not implement an appropriate behavioral intervention plan was ordered to reimburse the parent for the costs of the student's out-of-state residential placement in *Stroudsburg Area School District*, 27 IDELR 975 (SEA Pa. 1997).

A hearing officer annulled the expulsion of a 16-year-old special education student for his involvement in an alleged sexual assault because the district did not provide

---

*Functional Behavioral Assessment and Behavioral Intervention Plans, Technical Assistance Paper, Florida Department of Education, FY 1999-3D, June, 1998.

the student with a behavioral intervention plan in *Hacienda La Puente Unified School District,* 30 IDELR 105 (SEA CA 1999)

It is important to note, however, that in *Horry County School District v. P.F.,* 29 IDELR 354 (D.S.C. 1998), the court stated that a school is not compelled to "exhaust all heroic or possible methods" to minimize a student's behavior, and, further that IDEA does not require that all conceivable interventions to minimize the risk of harm be made.

Manifestation Determination Review

"Self-control is the quality that distinguishes the fittest to survive."

George Bernard Shaw

The term "manifestation determination" means the evaluation of the relationship between a student's disability and acts of misconduct that must be undertaken when a school proposes to take specified serious disciplinary actions. 20 U.S.C. 1415 (k) (4) Only if the school concludes, after performing a manifestation determination review, that the misconduct was not related to the student's disability can it impose the proposed disciplinary sanction. Manifestation determinations, and the IEP team meeting to make the determination, are ONLY required when a child is subjected to a disciplinary change of placement. 34 C.F.R. 300.523 When the cumulative total day suspension is less than 10 days, a manifestation determination hearing is not required. *Metropolitan Nashville (TN) Public Schools,* 29 IDELR

488 (OCR 1998) However, a manifestation determination hearing must be conducted whenever a suspension of more than 10 days is contemplated. *Fairfax County Public Schools,* 29 IDELR 1008 (SEA VA 1998)

When a student was only suspended for three days and had no other suspensions during the school year, no manifestation determination review hearing was required. *Northeast Independent School District,* 28 IDELR 1004 (SEA TX 1998) If a disciplinary action involving a change of placement for more than 10 days is contemplated for a child with a disability who has engaged in behavior that violated any rule that applies to all children, not later than the date on which the decision to take that action is made, the parents shall be notified of that decision and of all procedural safeguards afforded. Immediately, if possible, but in no case later than 10 school days after the date on which the decision to take that action is made, a review shall be conducted of the relationship between the child's disability and the behavior subject to the disciplinary action. The review shall be conducted by the IEP Team and other qualified personnel. In carrying out the review, the IEP Team may determine that the behavior of the child was not a manifestation of such child's disability only if the IEP Team:

> ***Noteworthy***
>
> Manifestation determination reviews determine the relationship between a student's disability and his acts of misconduct.

(1) first considers, in terms of the behavior subject to disciplinary action, all relevant information, including

   (a) evaluation and diagnostic results, including such results or other relevant information supplied by the parents of the child;

   (b) observations of the child; and

   (c) the child's IEP and placement; and

(2) then determines that

   (a) in relationship to the behavior subject to disciplinary action, the child's IEP and placement were appropriate and the special education services, supplementary aids and services, and behavior intervention strategies were provided consistent with the child's IEP and placement;

   (b) the child's disability did not impair the ability of the child to understand the impact and consequences of the behavior subject to disciplinary action; and

   (c) the child's disability did not impair the ability of the child to control the behavior subject to disciplinary action. 20 U.S.C. 1415 (k) (4); 34 C.F.R. 300.523

If the student's disability has no impact on his judgment or on his ability to regulate his behavior, the behavior is not a manifestation of his disability. *In Re: Student with a Disability,* 30 **IDELR** 113 (SEA CT 1999)

If the result of the manifestation determination review is a determination that the behavior of the child was not a manifestation of his disability, the relevant disciplinary procedures applicable to children without disabilities may be applied to the child. 20 U.S.C. 1415 (k) (5) (A); 34 C.F.R. 300.524 (a)

If the school expels a student without first conducting a manifestation determination review, compensatory education may be awarded to the parents. *Ashland Sch. Dist.*, 28 IDELR 630 (SEA Ore. 1998)

The manifestation review may be conducted at the same meeting that is convened to address the functional behavioral assessment/behavioral intervention plan. 34 C.F.R. 300.523 (e) If, at the manifestation review, a school identifies any deficiencies in the child's IEP or in the child's placement, the school must make immediate steps to remedy those deficiencies. 34 C.F.R. 300.523 (f)

If a child's parent disagrees with a determination that the child's behavior was not a manifestation of the child's disability, the parent may request a hearing. 20 U.S.C. 1415 (k) (6) (A) (i); 34 C.F.R. 300.525 (a) (1) "Stay put" applies. 34 C.F.R. 300.524 (c)

Entitlement to Protections

A child who has not been determined to be eligible for special education and related services and who has engaged in behavior that violates any rule or code of conduct, may assert any of the protections of IDEA if the school had knowledge that the child was a child with a disability before the behavior that precipitated the disciplinary action occurred.

A school shall be deemed to have knowledge that a child is a child with a disability if:

(1) The parent has expressed concern in writing (unless the parent is illiterate or has a disability that prevents it) to personnel of the appropriate educational agency that the child is in need of special education and related services;

(2) The behavior or performance of the child demonstrates the need for such services;

(3) The parent has requested an evaluation under the IDEA;

(4) The teacher of the child, or other personnel of the school, has expressed concern about the behavior or performance of the child to the director of special education of such agency or to other personnel of the agency. 34 C.F.R. 300.527 (b)

IDEA does not provide any set timeframe for determining whether a school district knew or should have known that a student was disabled. IDEA further does not limit what evidence can be considered when determining whether a district knew or should have known that a student was a student with a disability. *North Pocono School District*, 29 IDELR 111 (SEA PA 1998)

A school would not be deemed to have knowledge if, as a result of receiving the required information, the school either conducted an evaluation and determined that the child was not a child with a disability, or determined that an evaluation was not necessary, and provided notice to the child's parent of its determination.

If a request is made for an evaluation of a child during the time period in which the child is subjected to disciplinary measures, the evaluation must be conducted in an expedited manner. Until the evaluation is completed, the child remains in the educational placement determined by the school, which can include suspension or expulsion without educational services.

A Maryland appeals court rejected a challenge to a high school student's expulsion, finding that even though the student might have attention deficit hyperactivity disorder, there was no indication the student was eligible for special education services. Accordingly, the student was not entitled to the additional protections provided to students with disabilities. *Miller v. Board of Educ. Of Caroline County*, 25 IDELR 811 (Md. Ct. Spec. App. 1997)

Inmate Services

All children with disabilities aged 3 through 21 have the right to FAPE, including children with disabilities who have been suspended or expelled from school. 34 C.F.R. 300.121 (a) The obligation to provide FAPE to students aged 18 through 21 does not apply to the extent that State law does not require that special education and related services be provided to a student with a disability who, in the last educational placement prior to his incarceration in an adult correctional facility, was not actually identified as being a child with a disability and did not have an IEP. 34 C.F.R. 300.311 (a)

The requirements for participation in assessments and transitional planning and services do not apply to students with disabilities who are convicted as adults and incarcerated in adult prisons. In addition, the IEP team may modify the student's IEP or placement if the State has demonstrated a bona fide security or compelling penological interest that cannot otherwise be accommodated. 34 C.F.R. 300.311 (b) (c)

In *Rodiriecus L. v. Waukegan Sch. Dist.*, 24 IDELRR 563 (7th Cir., 1996), the Court held that the stay-put rule does not apply to students who are not previously diagnosed as disabled under IDEA unless the school knew or reasonably should have known that the child was eligible for special education.

Referral to Law Enforcement

Nothing in the law prohibits a school from reporting a crime. As a matter of fact, school officials are to report crimes committed by children with disabilities to appropriate law enforcement authorities to the same extent as they do for crimes committed by nondisabled students. 34 C.F.R. 300.529

A school reporting a crime may transmit copies of the child's special education and disciplinary records only to the extent that the transmission is permitted by the Family Educational Rights and Privacy Act. 34 C.F.R. 300.529

Student Artist: Justin Bohley
Pine Ridge Middle School, Naples, Florida
Teachers: Carol Mullen and Danielle Yarusevich

Chapter 9

Procedural Safeguards

"Be able to perceive what the issues are before they become issues."
                              Stewart Alsop III

Written Notice

Written notice is required whenever the school proposes or refuses to initiate or change the identification, evaluation, or educational placement of the child. 20 U.S.C. 1415 (b) (3) Written notice is also required whenever there is a change of placement for discipline, a change of placement when a special education student will graduate from high school with a regular diploma and whenever there is a manifestation determination review scheduled. 34 C.F.R. 300.504 A copy of the procedural safe-

> ***Noteworthy***
>
> All of the procedural safeguards should be provided in the notice.

guards available to the parents of a child with a disability shall be given to the parents upon initial referral for evaluation, upon each notification of an individual education program meeting, upon re-evaluation of the child, and upon registration of a complaint. U.S.C. 20 1415 (d) (1); 34 C.F.R. 300.504 (a)

Content of the Notice

The procedural safeguards notice shall include a full explanation of the procedural safeguards, written in the native language of the parents (unless it clearly is not feasible to do so), and written in an clearly understandable manner, relating to:

(1) *Independent educational evaluation;*

(2) *Prior written notice;*

(3) *Parental consent;*

(4) *Access to all educational records;*

(5) *Opportunity to present complaints;*

(6) *The child's placement during pendency of due process proceedings;*

(7) *Procedures for students who are subject to placement in an interim alternative educational setting;*

(8) *Requirements for unilateral placement by parents of children in private schools at public expense;*

(9) *Mediation;*

(10) *Due process hearings,* including requirements for disclosure of evaluation results and recommendations.

(11) *State-level appeals;*

(12) *Civil actions;*

(13) *Attorneys' fees;*
 20 U.S.C. 1415; (d) (2)

(14) *The state complaint procedures* including a description of how to file a complaint and the timelines under those procedures; 34 C.F.R. 300.504 (b) (14)

(15) *The ability of either party to invite individuals with knowledge or special expertise* to the meeting. 34 C.F.R. 300.345 (b) (ii)

Note that procedural violations do not necessarily deprive a student of FAPE unless the procedural inadequacies result in the loss of educational opportunity or seriously infringe upon the parents' opportunity to participate in the IEP formulation process. *Board of Trustees of Target Range School District No. 23,* 18 IDELR 1019 (9th Cir., 1992)

Transfer of Rights

States may decide to transfer all rights to a child with disabilities when the child reaches the age of majority under state law (except for a child with disabilities who has been determined to be incompetent, or who is determined not to have the ability to provide informed consent with respect to his educational program). 20 U.S.C. 1415 (m) The

> **Noteworthy**
>
> Rights can be transferred to a student when he attains majority.

school shall provide notice to both the child and the parents and all other rights accorded to parents transfer to the child. 34 C.F.R. 300.517 (a)

If a State has a mechanism to determine that a student with a disability, who has reached the age of majority under State law and has not been determined incompetent under State law, does not have the ability to provide informed consent with respect to his or her educational program, the State shall establish procedures for appointing the parent, or, if the parent is not available, another appropriate individual, to represent the educational interests of the student throughout the student's eligibility. 34 C.F.R. 300.517 (b)

> **Noteworthy**
>
> Written notice is required whenever a school proposes or refuses to initiate or change the identification, evaluation or placement of the child.

In addition, all rights accorded to parents transfer to students who are incarcerated in adult or juvenile, State or local correctional institutions. 34 C.F.R. 300.517 (a)

Graduation

A student's right to FAPE is terminated upon graduation with a regular high school diploma, but is not terminated by any other kind of graduation certificate or diploma. *Daugherty by Daugherty v. Hamilton County Schs.*, 26 **IDELR** 127 (E.D. Tenn. 1997)

Written prior notice is required because graduation

Procedural Safeguards

with a high school regular diploma constitutes a change in placement. 34 C.F.R 300.122 (a) (3) The notice should be provided a reasonable time before proposing to graduate a student in order to ensure that there is sufficient time for the parents and student to plan for, or challenge, the pending graduation. Evaluation is not required before graduation. Once a student graduates, the school's obligation under IDEA for FAPE to the student ends. 34 C.F.R. 300.534 (c)

*Artwork from students at
Lake Park Elementary School, Naples, Florida
Teacher: Dini Melko*

Chapter 10

Mediation

"In negotiating, it's important to practice the art of discretion, which simply means raising your eyebrow instead of your voice."

Myers Barnes

Mediation must be available whenever a Due Process Hearing is requested. The procedures for mediation ensure that the process is voluntary on the part of the parties and is conducted by a qualified and impartial mediator who is trained in effective mediation techniques. 20 U.S.C. 1415 (e) (2); 34 C.F.R. 300.506

Any agreement reached by the parties in the mediation process must be set forth in a written mediation agreement.

Noteworthy

Mediation is available when there is a due process requested.

If an agreement is reached during mediation, the parents cannot later challenge it. By signing the mediation agreement, the parents have consented to the offered service as appropriate. *Independent School District No. 281 (Robbinsdale)*, 28 IDELR 370 (SEA MN 1998)

> **Noteworthy**
>
> Mediation is voluntary, but advisable.

Discussions that occur during mediation are confidential and may not be used as evidence in any subsequent due process hearing. Attorneys are not barred, but cannot recover attorney's fees for participation in mediation. Every effort should be made to resolve differences between parents and school staff through voluntary mediation without resorting to a due process hearing. However, mediation or other informal procedures may not be used to deny or delay a parent's right to a due process hearing. 34 C.F.R. 300.506

A school may establish procedures to require parents who elect not to use the mediation process to meet, at a time and location convenient to the parents, with a disinterested party who is under contract with a parent training and information center or community parent resource center or an appropriate alternative dispute resolution entity and who would explain the benefits of the mediation process, and encourage the parents to use the process. While the school may require that

> **Noteworthy**
>
> Mediation agreements must be in writing to be enforceable.

Mediation

the parent attend the meeting to receive an explanation of the benefits of mediation and to encourage its use, a parent's failure to attend this meeting prior to the due process hearing should not be used to justify delay or denial of the hearing or the hearing decision. 34 C.F.R. 300.506

*Artwork from students at
Lake Park Elementary School, Naples, Florida
Teacher: Dini Melko*

Chapter 11

Due Process Hearings

"Choose your battles wisely."   Unknown

Whenever a complaint has been received, the parents involved in such complaint shall have an opportunity for an impartial due process hearing, which shall be conducted by the State or local educational agency, as determined by State law. 20 U.S.C. 1415 (f) The Eleventh Amendment to the U.S. Constitution, which bars citizens from bringing suits against their own state in federal courts, does not apply to IDEA actions. *Little Rock School District v. Mauney*, 30 IDELR 668 (8th Cir. 1999)

Due process hearings have become increasingly sophisticated, complex and costly. Due process hearings can also be very contentious, as parties fight a "war over the future welfare . . . of the student." *Sherri A.D. v. Kirby*, 19 IDELR 339 (5th Cir. 1992)

Although each state's particular system for deciding special education disputes may be different, many common elements exist. Every state must establish a timeline for expedited due process hearings that results in a written decision being mailed to the parties within 45 days of the school's receipt of the request for the hearing, without exceptions or extensions. The timeline must be the same for hearings requested by parents or schools. 34 C.F.R. 300.528

> **Noteworthy**
>
> Due process hearings are completed within 45 days of the school's receipt of request.

The school must have procedures that require the parents of a child with a disability or the attorney representing the child to provide notice (which must remain confidential) to the school in a request for a hearing that contains: (1) the name of the child; (2) the address of the residence of the child; (3) the name of the school the child is attending; (4) a description of the nature of the problem of the child relating to the proposed or refused initiation or change, including facts relating to the problem; and (5) a proposed resolution of the problem to the extent known and available to the parents at the time. 34 C.F.R. 300.507 (c)

Parties involved in the due process hearing have the following rights:

(1) to be accompanied and advised by legal counsel and by individuals with special knowledge or training with respect to the problems of children with disabilities;

(2) to present evidence and confront, cross-examine and compel the attendance of witnesses;

(3) the right to a written or, at the option of the parents, electronic verbatim record of the hearing; and

(4) the right to written or, at the option of the parents, electronic findings of fact and decisions. 20 U.S.C. 1415 (h)

If the hearing is conducted by the school district in a state with a two-tier administrative procedure, any party aggrieved by the outcome of the hearing may appeal to the state educational agency which conducts an impartial review of the hearing decision. The officer conducting the review shall make an independent decision upon completion of the review. 20 U.S.C. 1415 (g)

Any party aggrieved by the findings and decision made pursuant to the due process hearing procedure has the right to bring a civil action in any state court of competent jurisdiction or in federal district court. 20 U.S.C. 1415 (i) (2) The proceeding in court is not completely *de novo* as the court is required to receive the records of the administrative proceedings, to hear additional evidence at the request of a party, and to make a decision based on a preponderance of the evidence. 20 U.S.C. 1415 (i) (2) (B) "Additional evidence" means supplemental evidence and does not authorize a witness to repeat or embellish prior hearing testimony. *Ojai Unified Sch. Dist. v. Jackson,* 20 IDELR 354 (9th Cir. 1993)

> **Noteworthy**
>
> A hearing officer's decision may be appealed.

Regardless of whether the school or the parent initiated the procedures leading to the due process hearing, the same preparation should be taken. The school must substantiate by competent evidence that the position taken by the school is appropriate in light of IDEA and the Regulations.

The burden of proof rests with the party who attacks the IEP. *Logue by Logue v. Shawnee Mission Public Sch. Unified School Dist. No. 512,* 25 IDELR 587 (SEA Kansas, 1997)

A school failed to meet its burden in establishing that it offered the student FAPE when it failed to enter a copy of the student's current IEP into evidence. *Board of Education of the Pittsford Central School Dist.,* 29 IDELR 653 (SEA NY 1998)

Records must be obtained, reviewed, and organized and should be assembled and indexed in a logical and chronological sequence. Witnesses should be identified, interviewed and prepared for their testimony. The witnesses must familiarize themselves with the documents that they will refer to in their respective testimony and which will be introduced into evidence through them. Issues need to be defined as narrowly as possible for the hearing officer.

A sequence of events in the hearing is likely to be as follows:

(1) Hearing Officer opening statement

(2) preliminary matters

(3) opening statements by the school's attorney and the parent's attorney

(4) presentation of school/parent case

(5) cross examination by the other side

(6) presentation of school/parent case

(7) cross examination by the other side

(8) closing statements by the school's attorney and the parent's attorney

(9) arrangements for filing written briefs

(10) written final decision

(11) appeal

The hearing officer can limit the witnesses to those who have relevant testimony. *Board of Education of the Jericho Union Free School District,* 29 IDELR 135 (SEA NY 1998) The evidence can also be limited to relevant matters. *Board of Education of the City School District of the City of New York,* 27 IDELR 1000 (SEA NY 1998). For example, a due process hearing was not the appropriate forum for addressing the parents' contention that the student's educational records were inaccurate in *Dallas Independent School District,* 29 IDELR 930 (SEA TX 1998). A due process hearing was the incorrect forum for resolving the parents' request that the students' records be modified. *Board of Education of the Averill Park Central School District,* 27 IDELR 996 (SEA N.Y. 1998)

> **Noteworthy**
>
> The trial rules of procedure are relaxed somewhat in a due process hearing.

The hearing officer may limit repetitious testimony. *Board of Education of the Canastota Central School District,* 27 IDELR 419 (SEA NY 1997) The hearing officer may allow the admission of additional evidence, especially if it does not affect the outcome of the proceedings. *Judith S. v. Board of Education of Community Unit School District No. 200,* 28 IDELR 728 (ND Ill. 1998)

If the issues have been addressed at a previous due process hearing, res judicata bars further consideration of those same issues. *Dallas Independent School District,* 29 IDELR 930 (SEA TX 1998) In addition, if a settlement agreement has been reached which resolved the parties' dispute, that issue is not subject to review by due process. *Pascoe v. Washington Central School District,* 29 IDELR 31 (S.D. NY 1998)

The hearing officer may deny the parents' request to allow a witness to testify by telephone. *Board of Education of the City School District of the City of Ithaca,* 28 IDELR 71 (SEA NY 1998) It is clear that IDEA allows parties to "confront, cross-examine and compel" the attendance of witnesses. *Walled Lake Consolidated Schools by Jones by Thomas,* 24 IDELR 738 (ED Mich. 1996)

Chapter 12

Attorneys' Fees

*"There are just two ways of spreading light;
to be the candle or the mirror that reflects it."*
Edith Wharton

In any action or proceeding brought under IDEA, the court, in its discretion, may award reasonable attorneys' fees as part of the cost to the parents of a child with a disability who is the prevailing party. 20 U.S.C. 1415 (i) (3) (B); 34 C.F.R. 300.513 (a) "Prevailing party" and "reasonable" are to be interpreted in a manner consistent with the U.S. Supreme Court's interpretation which indicates:

> The extent of a plaintiff's success is a crucial factor in determining the proper amount of an award of attorney's fees. Where the plaintiff has failed to prevail on a claim that is distinct in all respects from his successful claims, the hours spent on the unsuccessful claim should be excluded in

> **Noteworthy**
>
> Attorneys' fees may be awarded to the parents if they are the "prevailing parties."

considering the amount of a reasonable fee. Where a lawsuit consists of related claims, a plaintiff who has won substantial relief should not have his attorney's fees reduced simply because the district court did not adopt each contention raised. But where the parents achieved only limited success, the district court awards only fees that are reasonable in relation to the results obtained. *Hensley v. Eckerhart,* 461 U.S. 424 (1983)

Fees are based on rates prevailing in the community in which the action or proceeding arose for the kind and quality of services furnished. No bonus or multiplier may be used in calculating the fees awarded. U.S.C. 1415 (i) (3) (C)

A parent's request for an award of attorneys' fees will be denied if the parents have not succeeded in obtaining the requested relief in the due process hearing. *Mr. and Mrs. H. v. Region 14 Board of Education,* 30 IDELR 359 (D. Conn. 1999)

> **Noteworthy**
>
> Attorneys' fees are not allowed at IEP meetings or mediation.

Courts may reduce fees if the parent unreasonably protracted final resolution; if fees are unreasonable; and/or if the hearing request did not provide the appropriate information required by IDEA. However, these provisions shall not apply if the court finds that the school or state unrea-

Attorneys' Fees

sonable protracted the final resolution of the action. 20 U.S.C. 1415 (i) (3)

Attorneys' fees may not be awarded and related costs may not be reimbursed in any action or proceeding for services performed subsequent to the time of a written offer of settlement to a parent if:

> (1) the offer is made within the time prescribed by Rule 68 of the Federal Rules of Civil Procedure (10 days prior to the beginning of the trial) or, in the case of an administrative proceeding, at any time more than 10 days before the proceeding begins;
>
> (2) the offer is not accepted within 10 days; AND
>
> (3) the court or administrative hearing officer finds that the relief finally obtained by the parents is not more favorable to the parents than the offer of settlement. 20 U.S.C. 1415 (i) (3) (D)

> **Noteworthy**
>
> Attorneys' fees awarded must be reasonable.

Notwithstanding the above, an award of attorneys' fees and related costs may be made to a parent who is the prevailing party and who was substantially justified in rejecting the settlement offer. 20 U.S.C. 1415 (i) (3) (E)

Attorneys' fees may not be awarded for:

> (1) any meeting of the IEP team unless such meeting is convened as a result of an administrative proceeding or judicial action, or,

> (2) at the discretion of the State, for a mediation that is conducted prior to the filing of a complaint. 20 U.S.C. 1415 (i) (3) (D) (ii)

The comments in the Regulations indicate that the presence of the school's attorney at an IEP meeting could "contribute to a potentially adversarial atmosphere at the meeting." Furthermore, the presence of any attorney accompanying the parents at the IEP meeting "would not necessarily be in the best interests of the child." 34 C.F.R. Part 300, Appendix A, Question 29

Chapter 13

Damages

> *"Lawsuit mania—a continual craving to go to war against others, while considering yourself the injured party."*
>
> Casare Lombroso

IDEA provides that a court reviewing the findings and determination of a hearing officer "shall grant such relief as it determines is appropriate." 20 U.S.C. 1415 (i) (2) "Appropriate relief" was defined to include reimbursement for private school tuition where a school had failed to provide FAPE to a disabled child in *Hall by Hall v. Vance County Bd. of Educ.*, 774 F. 2d 629 (4th Cir. 1985) However, while the court stated that the IDEA permitted reimbursement, the court went on to say that the Act "did

> **Noteworthy**
>
> The Eleventh Amendment immunity provision does not apply to IDEA.

not create a private cause of action for damages for educational malpractice." *Vance*, 774 F. 2d at 633 n. 3.

Monetary damages are not available as a remedy under IDEA. *Humble Independent School District,* 29 IDELR 833 (SEA TX 1998) The court in *Charlie F. v. Board of Educ. Of Skokie Sch. Dist.*, 98 F. 3d 989 (7th Cir. 1996), 24 IDELR 1039, stated that awarding compensatory or punitive damages would transform IDEA into a remedy for pain and suffering, emotional distress and other consequential damages, and that would be inconsistent with the structure of the Act which strongly favors the provision of the restoration of educational rights.

> ***Noteworthy***
>
> Money damages are not allowed under IDEA for pain and suffering, emotional distress or loss of academic opportunity.

The Court ruled that "the failure to evaluate and identify a child as having a disability and the failure to provide an appropriate placement do not give rise to damages under IDEA" in *W.B. v. Matula,* 67 F. 3d 484, 23 IDELR 411 (3rd Cir. 1995). Parents may seek reimbursement for private placements under IDEA (*Gupta v. Montgomery County Public Schools,* 25 IDELR 115 (D. MD 1996)), but may not seek damages for physical illness and emotional distress caused by the school's allegedly incompetent and unprofessional failure to provide the student with an adequate education. *Fort Zumwalt School District v. Clynes, et. al.* 26 IDELR 172 (8th Cir. 1997) Simply put, pain and suffering, emotional distress and loss of academic opportunities will not give rise to a claim for monetary damages under IDEA. *Heidemann v. Rother,* 84 F. 3d 1021, 24 IDELR 167 (8th Cir. 1996)

Chapter 14

Charter Schools

"When a vision begins to form, everything changes."

Jeanne Dixon

The definition of "local educational agency" includes charter schools that are established under State law. 34 C.F.R. 300.18 (b) (2) The school district must serve children with disabilities attending those schools in the same manner as it serves children with disabilities in its other schools. 20 U.S.C. 1413 (a) (5) Children with disabilities who attend public charter schools and their parents retain all rights that they would possess in the regular school. 34 C.F.R. 300.312

> **Noteworthy**
>
> A public school must provide IDEA services to charter schools if the district receives funding and includes other public schools.

(a) If the public charter school is a school of the local school district that receives funding and includes other public schools, the local school district is responsible for seeing that the requirements of IDEA are met. 34 C.F.R. 300.312 (c)

Chapter 15

Children in Private Schools

"Learning is an active practice; we learn by doing."
George Bernard Shaw

School-Placed

The school must locate, identify and evaluate private school children with disabilities. 20 U.S.C. 1412 (a) (3) (A); 34 C.F.R. 300.451 A child with a disability who is placed in or referred to a private school or facility by a school district must be provided special education and related services in conformance with an IEP and at no cost to the parents. 34 C.F.R. 300.401 District-placed private school students have the same rights as students with disabilities who are placed within the district. *Letter to Burr,* 30 IDELR 146, OSEP 1998.

If necessary for the child to benefit from or participate in the services provided, a private school child with a disability must be provided transportation from the child's school to the child's home, to a site other than the private school; and from the service site to the private school, or to the child's home, depending on the timing of the services. The public school is not required to provide transportation from the child's home to the private school. 34 C.F.R. 300.456

Parentally Placed

The law does not require the school district to pay for the cost of education, including special education and related services, of a child with a disability at a private school or facility if the school made FAPE available to the child and the parents elected to place the child in a private school or facility. *Letter to McKethan*, 29 IDELR 907, OSEP 1998

> **Noteworthy**
>
> If the school refers a child to a private school, the public school district must provide services.

No private school child with a disability has an individual right to receive the special education and related services that the child would receive if enrolled in the public school system. 34 C.F.R. 300.454 (a); *Northwestern Lehigh School District*, 29 IDELR 940 (SEA PA 1999) The child is, instead, entitled to a "proportionate" share of federal funds. 34 C.F.R. 300.452 In *Foley v. Special Sch. Dist. of St. Louis*, 28

IDELR 874 (8th Cir., 1998), the Court denied on-site occupational therapy, physical therapy and language services to a parochial student stating that the "proportionate" funds did not provide the student with a right to special education, let alone, special education on private school premises.

Each public school shall consult, in a timely and meaningful way, with appropriate representatives of private school children with disabilities in light of the funding under 34 C.F.R. 300.453, the number of private school children with disabilities, the needs of private school children with disabilities, and their location to decide which children will receive services, what services will be provided and how and where the services will be provided. *Letter to McKethan,* 29 IDELR 907, OSEP, 1998

The public school shall make the final decisions with respect to the services to be provided to eligible private school children. The special education and related services may be provided to students on the premises of private, including parochial, schools. 20 U.S.C. 1412 (a) (10 (A); *Gooddall v. Stafford County Sch. Bd.,* 60 F. 3d 168, 22 IDELR 972 (4th Cir., 1995)

The school has the discretion to determine if it will provide on-site services to special education students. *Russman by Russman v. Sobol,* 28 IDELR 612 (2d Cir. 1998)

> **Noteworthy**
>
> If the parent unilaterally places a child in a private school, the child does not have the same rights to special education that he would if he were a public school student.

If services are to be provided, a services plan shall be developed for each private school child with a disability who will receive special education services. 34 C.F.R. 300.452 Any services provided to private school students must be comparable to those provided to students who attend public schools. *Letter to Rothman,* 30 **IDELR** 269 OSEP 1998

Disagreements between parents and public schools regarding the availability of appropriate programs and the question of financial responsibility are subject to due process procedures. If the parents of a child with a disability, who previously received special education and related services under the authority of a public school, enroll the child in a private school without the consent of or referral by the public school, a court or a hearing officer may require the school to reimburse the parents for the cost of that enrollment if the court or hearing officer finds that the school had not made **FAPE** available to the child in a timely manner prior to that enrollment and that the private placement is appropriate. A parental placement may be found to be appropriate by a hearing officer or a court even if it does not meet the State standards that apply to public education. 34 C.F.R. 300.403 (c)

Cases that have interpreted the law have centered around the public school's providing **FAPE** to the student. The school was not required to provide a hearing impaired student with a sign language interpreter at the parochial school in which he was voluntarily enrolled by his parents since the student was offered **FAPE** in *Cefalu ex. rel. Cefalu v. East Baton Rouge Parish Sch. Bd.*, 117 F. 3d 231 (5th Cir. 1997), 25 **IDELR** 142

A school district was not required to provide an instructional aide to a severely disabled girl attending a parochial school because "comparable" services were offered when the district offered an aide at a public school. *K.R. v. Anderson Community Sch. Dist.*, 26 IDELR 864 (7th Cir. 1997)

Due process procedures do not apply to private school students. Complaints that a school has failed to meet the requirements, including the provision of services indicated on the child's services plan, may be filed with the State Department using State complaint procedures. 34 C.F.R. 300.457 However, in one exceptional case a due process hearing was allowed to consider the provision of services to a unilaterally placed private school student. The 18-year-old hearing impaired student had been home-schooled for eight years and had an IEP which provided a range of services which were offered in the public school. Support for this position was found in an OSEP policy interpretation that due process rights "attach" and are "available to private school students with disabilities in situations where parents claim that their children are not receiving the special education services that the district has agreed to provide or that the services are not provided in the manner agreed to by the parties." In this instance, the due process was warranted since the district decided to service the student, and then refused to implement the IEP which was offered and substituted another IEP. *South Lyon Community School*, 30 IDELR 728 (SEA MI 1999)

Reimbursement for the costs of a unilateral private school placement may be reduced or denied if:

> ***Noteworthy***
>
> The private school student is entitled to a "proportionate" share of federal funds.

(1) At the most recent IEP meeting the parents did not inform the team that they were rejecting the proposed placement and intending to enroll the student in private school; or

(2) Ten business days prior to the removal of the child, the parent did not give written notice to the school of their intention to make the unilateral private placement; or

(3) Prior to removal, the school informed the parents of their intent to evaluate the child and the parents did not make the child available; or

(4) Upon a judicial finding of unreasonableness with respect to actions taken by the parents.

EXCEPT:

    (a) If the parent is illiterate and cannot write in English;

    (b) If compliance with the notice requirement would likely result in physical or serious emotional harm to the child;

    (c) If the school prevented the parent from providing notice; or

    (d) If the parents had not received notice from the school of their obligation to provide notice of their intent to make a unilateral private school placement.

U.S.C. 1412 (a) (10) (C)

I
AM
ME.
I
AM
SPECIAL.
I MAY ALWAYS BE A
SECOND BEST TO SOMEBODY ELSE
BUT
I
AM
THE
BEST
ME
THAT
THERE
IS.

Unknown

Afterword

"Preparation and collaboration—not litigation."
M. Jean Rawson

My thirty-plus years in education have reinforced my belief that most educators and parents are caring and well-meaning people. They want to do the right thing for special education students. They even want to do it the right way and for all the right reasons. Many, however, lack the preparation and knowledge to accomplish the desired goals in the correct manner. Difficulties arise when people's preconceived notions are only about their individual perspectives. Maybe some expectations are unrealistic—and maybe some circumstances won't fit a specific plan or idea.

The scenario is all too familiar. That predicament leads to frustration—which leads to misunderstanding—which then leads to litigation.

A knowledge of the law is only the beginning. Implementing that law in a cooperative fashion is the next necessary step for educators and parents serving special education students. Staff development programs about special education law are essential for schools. Parents must also organize, glean, and exchange information with educators in order for the necessary parties to collaborate in conceiving appropriate education programs for special education students. It's amazing what ordinary people can achieve if they set out with a knowledge of special education law in a sincere effort to provide an appropriate education for children with disabilities.

It is hoped that this book will serve to simplify complex legal issues and promote cooperation among all parties so that we may better serve children with disabilities. We must all "become the change we seek in the world." (M. Ghandi)

Index

Accommodations, 38
Accountability, 51
Alternative educational program, 61
Amanda S. by Susan S. v. Webster City Community School District, 27 IDELR 698 (N.D. Iowa 1998), 43
Appeal, 95
Assessments, 38, 23, 40
Ashland Sch. Dist., 28 IDELR 630 (SEA Ore. 1998), 78
Assistive technology device, 5
Assistive technology service, 6
Attorneys' fees, 99

Behavioral intervention plan, 70
Bd. of Educ. Of the Akron Central Sch. Dist, 28 IDELR 909 (SEA NY 1998), 66, 70
Board of Education of the Averill Park Central School District, 27 IDELR 996 (SEA N.Y. 1998), 97

Board of Education of the Canastota Central School District, 27 IDELR 419 (SEA NY 1997), 97
Board of Education of the City School District of the City of Ithaca, 28 IDELR 71 (SEA NY 1998), 98
Board of Education of the City School District of the City of New York, 27 IDELR 1000 (SEA NY 1998), 97
Board of Education of the Jericho Union Free School District, 29 IDELR 135 (SEA NY 1998), 97
Board of Education of the Pittsford Central School Dist., 29 IDELR 653 (SEA NY 1998), 96
Board of Education of the Roslyn Union Free School District, 27 IDELR 1113 (SEA NY 1998), 15
Board of Education v. Rowley, 458

U.S. 176 (1982), 102 S. Ct.3034, 2
Board of Educ. of the Victor Central Sch. Dist., 27 IDELR 1159 (SEA NY 1998), 29
Board of Trustees of Target Range Sch. Dist. No. 23, 18 IDELR 1019 (9th Cir., 1992), 85
Brent v. San Diego Unified Sch. Dist., 25 IDELR 344 (S.D. Calif. 1996), 15
Buncombe County Sch. Dist., 23 IDELR 364 (OCR 1995), 60

Cedar Rapids Community School District v. Garret F. (No. 96-1793, decided March 3, 1999), 14
Cefalu ex. rel. Cefalu v. East Baton Rouge Parish Sch. Bd., 117 F. 3d 231 (5th Cir. 1997), 25 IDELR 142, 110
Change in placement, 59
Charlie F. v. Board of Educ. of Skokie Sch. Dist., 98 F. 3d 989 (7th Cir. 1996), 24 IDELR 1039, 104
Charter schools, 105
Child find, 21
Child with a disability, 7, 47
Community Consolidated School District 15, 30 IDELR 448, (SEA IL, 1999), 65
Community Consolidated School Dist. No. 180, 27 IDELR 1004 (SEA Ill. 1998), 30
Consensus, 48

Consent, 8, 25, 27
Cronkite v. Long Beach Unified Sch. Dist., 30 IDELR 510 (9th Cir., 1999), 51

Dallas School District, 28 IDELR 1225 (SEA TX 1998), 98
Dallas Independent School District, 29 IDELR 930 (SEA TX 1998), 97
Damages, 103
Daugherty by Daugherty v. Hamilton County Schs., 26 IDELR 127 (E.D. Tenn. 1997), 86
Day, 9
Devine Independent School District, 25 IDELR 1238 (SEA Tex. 1997), 74
Discipline, 59
District of Columbia Public Schools, 28 IDELR 401 (SEA D.C. 1998), 60
Due process hearings, 93

Educational records, 35, 50
Eleventh Amendment (immunity), 103
Eligibility, 31
Evaluation, 23, 87
Extended school year, 9

Fairfax County Public Schools, 29 IDELR 1008 (SEA VA 1998), 76
Family Educational Rights & Privacy Act (FERPA), 35, 50, 81

Index

Free appropriate public education (FAPE), 10
Foley v. Special Sch. Dist. of St. Louis, 28 IDELR 874 (8th Cir., 1998), 108
Freeport Public Schools, 26 IDELR 1251 (SEA ME 1997), 66, 74
Fort Zumwalt School District v. Clynes, et. al. 26 IDELR 172 (8th Cir. 1997), 104
Functional behavior analysis, 67

Gadsden City Board of Education v. B. P., 28 IDELR 166 (N.D. Ala. 1998), 64
General curriculum, 11, 38, 46
Goals, 37, 47
Goodall v. Stafford County Sch. Bd., 60 F. 3d 168, 22 IDELR 972 (4th Cir., 1995), 109
Graduation, 83, 86
Greenbush Sch. Committee v. Mr. And Mrs. K. ex. rel. JK, 26 IDELR 200 (D. Me. 1996), 41
Gupta v. Montgomery County Public Schools, 25 IDELR 115 (D. MD 1996), 104
Gwinnett Country School System, 4 ECLPR, Sec. 98 (SEA Ga., 1999), 43

Hacienda La Puente Unified School District, 30 IDELR 105 (SEA CA 1999), 73

Hall by Hall v. Vance County Bd. of Educ., 774 F. 2d 629 (4th Cir. 1985), 65, 103
Hart, William S. Union High Sch. Dist., 26 IDELR 1258 (SEA CA 1997), 69
Hartmann by Hartmann v. Loudoun County Bd. of Educ., 26 IDELR 167 (4th Cir. 1997), 13
Heidemann v. Rother, 84 F. 3d 1021, 24 IDELR 167 (8th Cir. 1996), 104
Hensley v. Eckerhart, 461 U.S. 424 (1983), 100
Highland Local Sch. Dist., 26 IDELR 224 (SEA Ohio 1997), 16
Honig v. Doe, EHLR 559:231 (1988), 64
Horry County School District v. P.F., 29 IDELR 354 (D.S.C. 1998), 75
Humble Independent School District, 29 IDELR 833 (SEA TX 1998), 107
Hudson by Hudson v. Bloomfield Hills Pub. Schs., 26 IDELR 607 (6th Cir. 1997), 13

Identification, 21
Incarcerated students, 80
Independent education evaluation (IEE), 28
Independent School District No. 281 (Robbinsdale), 28 IDELR 340 (SEA MN 1998), 90

Independent School Dist. No. 2310, 29 IDELR 330 (SEA MN 1998), 68, 70
Independent School Dist No. 279, Osseo Area School, 30 IDELR 645 (SEA MN 1999), 65
Individualized education program (IEP), 12, 35, 47
IEP meetings, 48, 49
IEP team, 41, 47
Inmate services, 80
In Re: Student with a Disability, 30 IDELR 113 (SEA CT 1999), 77
Interim alternative placement (setting), 61
Irving Independent School District v. Tatro (468 U.S. 883 (1984)), 13

Judith S. v. Board of Education of Community Unit School District No. 200, 28 IDELR 728 (ND Ill. 1998), 97

K.R. v. Anderson Community Sch. Dist., 26 IDELR 864 (7th Cir. 1997), 111
Kari H. v. Franklin Spec. Sch. Dist, 16 IDELR 569 (6th Cir. 1997), 12

Least restrictive environment. 12, 56
Letter to Anonymous, 30 IDELR 538 (OSEP 1998), 32
Letter to Bachman, 29 IDELR 1092 (OSEP, 1997), 63
Letter to Blades, 213:169, OSERS, 1988, 49, 50
Letter to Burr, 30 IDELR 146, OSEP 1998, 107
Letter to Collins, 30 IDELR 404 (OSEP 1998), 46
Letter to Kleczka, 30 IDELR 270 (OSEP 1998), 9
Letter to Hale, 30 IDELR 142 (OSEP 1997), 58
Letter to McKethan, 29 IDELR 907, OSEP 1998, 108, 109
Letter to Rothman, 30 IDELR 269, OSEP 1998, 110
Letter to Slatkin, 213:128, OSERS 1998, 48
Letter to Smith, 23 IDELR 344 (OSEP 1995), 15
Lewisville Independent Sch. Dist., 28 IDELR 1024 (SEA TX 1998), 28
Little Rock School District v. Mauney, 30 IDELR 668 (8th Cir. 1999), 93
Local educational agency, 45, 105
Long Beach Unified School Dist., 28 IDELR 777 (SEA CA 1998), 29
Logue by Logue v. Shawnee Mission Public Schs. Unified Sch. Dist. No. 512, 25 IDELR 587 (SEA Kan. 1997), 96

McMillan by Collins v. Cheatham County Schools, 25 IDELR 398 (M.D. Tenn. 1997), 47

Index

Malehorn v. Hill City Sch. Dist., 27 IDELR 144 (S.D. 1997), 16
Manifestation determination hearing, 75
Mediation, 89
Medical services, 13
Metropolitan Nashville (TN) Public Schools, 29 IDELR 488 (OCR 1998), 75
Miller v. Board of Educ. of Caroline County, 25 IDELR 811 (Md. Ct. Spec. App. 1997), 80
Modifications, 38
Morris by Morris v. Metropolitan Gov't of Nashville and Davidson County, 26 IDELR 159 (M.D. Tenn. 1997), 56
Mr. and Mrs. H.v. Region Board of Education, 30 IDELR 359 (D. Conn. 1999), 100

Northeast Independent School District, 28 IDELR 1004 (SEA TX 1998), 76
Northwestern Lehigh School District, 29 IDELR 940 (SEA PA 1999), 108
North Pocono School District, 29 IDELR 111 (SEA PA 1998), 79
Notice, 83, 86

Oberti v. Clemson Sch. Dist., 995 F. 2d 1204 (3rd Cir., 1993), 19 IDELR 908, 57

Objectives, 37
Ojai Unified Sch. Dist. v. Jackson, 4 F. 3d 1467, 20 IDELR 354 (9th Cir. 1993), 95
Oregon City School Dist., 28 IDELR 96 (SEA OR 1998), 66
Oregon City Sch. District 62, 28 IDELR 536 (SEA OR 1998), 28
Other health impairment, 7
O'Toole by O'Toole v. Olathe District Sch. Unified Sch. District No. 233, 28 IDELR 177 (10th Cir., 1998) 36, 41, 51, 52

Parents, 41
Pascoe v. Washington Central School District, 29 IDELR 31 (S.D. NY 1998), 98
Pattern of removals, 59
Physical education, 16
Placement, 55
Pottstown School District, 30 IDELR 651 (SEA PA 1999), 62, 67
Prevailing party, 99
Present level of educational performance, 36
Private schools, 107
Procedural safeguards, 83
Protections (of IDEA), 78

Recording devices, 50
Re-evaluation, 25
Referral to law enforcement, 81

Regular education teacher, 43
Related services, 13, 43
Reports to parents, 53
Ridgewood Bd. Of Educ. v. N.E., 30 IDELR 41 (3d Cir. 1999), 11
Rodiriecus L. v. Waukegan Sch. Dist., 24 IDELR 563 (7th Cir., 1996), 81
Russman by Russman v. Mills, 28 IDELR 612 (2d Cir. 1998), 109

San Antonio Independent Sch. Dist., 29 IDELR 630 (SEA TX 1998), 29
San Diego Unified Sch. Dist., 28 IDELR 244 (SEA CS 1998), 15
Searcy Public Schools, 30 IDELR 825 (SEA AR 1999), 44
Shasta Union H.S. Dist., 30 IDELR 733 (SEA CA 1999), 28
Sherri A.D. v. Kirby, 19 IDELR 339 (5th Cir. 1992), 93
Sherry v. New York State Educ. Dept. 479 F. Supp. 1328 (W.D.N.Y. 1979), 60
South Lyon Community School, 30 IDELR 728 (SEA MI 1999), 111
Special education teacher, 45
Specially-designed instruction, 17
Special education, 16

Stay put, 17, 65, 78, 81
Stroudsburg Area School District, 27 IDELR 975 (SEA Pa. 1997), 74
Substantial evidence, 62
Supplementary aids and services, 17, 38
Suspension, 60, 75

Three Rivers/Josephine County School District, 28 IDELR 1228 (SEA OR 1998), 43
Transfer of rights, 39, 85
Transition services, 19, 39, 47
Transportation, 15
Travel training, 17
Tuscaloosa County School Board, 30 IDELR 842 (SEA AL 1999), 52
Tucson Unified Sch. Dist., 30 IDELR 478 (SEA Ariz., 1999), 52

Vocational education, 17

W.B. v. Matula, 67 F. 3d 484, 23 IDELR 411 (3rd Cir. 1995), 104
Walled Lake Consolidated Schools by Jones by Thomas, 24 IDELR 738 (ED Mich. 1996), 98
Weapon, 62
West Contra Costa Unified School District, 28 IDELR 802 (SEA CA 1998), 29

ORDER FORM

A Manual of Special Education Law
for Educators and Parents
M. Jean Rawson, ESQ.

$17.95 per book.

Discount available for orders of 10 or more books; contact Publisher for details.

Florida residents add 6% sales tax.

Add shipping costs of $1.50 for one book; $3.50 for 2–10 books.

Please send _____ copies at 17.95 per copy

Subtotal _____

Tax (6% within Florida) _____

Shipping ($1.50 for one book; $3.50 for 2–10) _____

TOTAL _____

____ Check/Money Order payable to Morgen Publishing, Inc. is enclosed

Name _____

Street _____

City/State/Zip _____

Send form and check or money order to:

Morgen Publishing, Inc.
P. O. Box 754
Naples, Florida 34102

Call 941-263-8206

Fax 941-263-8472